I want to b

Klopp

and other strange thoughts about football

By Oscar Oberg

Text copyright © 2015 by Oscar Oberg

All rights reserved

Cover design by Wootikom Hanroog

1 Warm up.

I am somewhat lazy. I am not ashamed of that; it is what it is, but it affects my way of writing. Due to my laziness, I will try to keep this introduction short, because I believe that the texts that come after this introduction are more interesting to the reader.

But first, I can tell you the purpose of this book, without being too detailed. This is a collection of essays based on football (and yes, by football I mean real football - not the American version), but they are essays that will explore and discuss concepts that I tend to ponder in my daily life. I have always been interested in how to connect the different parts of my life to other parts of my life together - how to relate to other people by my own passions - because the world isn't that very different whether you are dealing with football or acting (especially in the case of Arjen Robben). I have often tried to explain this attitude in conversations, often with the result of being perceived as a football geek (notably an Arsenal one). Being sentenced to geekdom would in no way be a problem if the term "football geek" meant "a person who is deeply passionate about the complex and spiritually rewarding art football," but most people, unfortunately, think a football geek is synonymous with "a mentally inferior person who long ago ceased to pursue any sort of personal development." I've noticed that in the written form, all this becomes clearer

I don't think the only reason I'm writing this book is to explain the greatness of football, even though throughout this book I will have enough time to offer one or two over-the-top-tributes to this incredibly beautiful sport. Rather I believe that the biggest reason why these essays have seen the light of day is that I simply thought it was fun to write them. Fun should always be the main reason for writing. It's amazingly fun for me that a quote from Bill Burr can serve as an entry door to the world of football tactics or that Stuart Pearce can be discussed by references to punk and Johnny Rotten. I can't pretend to be amused playing around with ideas that I don't really like; it doesn't work for me. As you will see, I try to be funny sometimes, and sometimes my tone seems a little bit angry. That isn't a well-formed strategy, it's just that sometimes I think I'm funny and sometimes I'm upset about something. Simple math. However, I hope you feel that I'm honest, engaging, and somehow interesting no matter what mood I had when I wrote the text; for me, that is absolutely the most important thing.

Before we finish the introduction, I would like to thank my lovely and talented family, who read the book and provided loads of valuable comments and suggestions. They have called me out when I was too arrogant in my arguments, or when I was a little bit too childish in my expressions. Of course I don't want to remove all those parts because sometimes I am a bit arrogant and childish, and I think to some extent that should be reflected in the text. It can be good for everyone – if there's not too much of it. Also, I want to thank Noelia and Franscesco, the owners of the hostel Blablabla Tasarte in Gran Canaria, where most of my essays were written. They have incredibly big hearts.

They presented me with the most perfect writing room for a couple of months, and it feels good to thank them even though I don't know if they will ever read this.

But anyway, now I'm a little impatient. Let's move on.

2 A beautiful mind.

I read Jay-Z's wonderful book *Decoded*, when I came across a quote, which I think is a good introduction to this text: "That which distinguished the best rappers of the '80s was that they looked very carefully at the world, and then described it in an extremely skillful and intelligent manner." Details. It's all about details.

I remember when I was younger and reading Sherlock Holmes. There was something about the book that struck a nerve in me. I don't think it was just the story itself – I had read and seen similar stories before – and I don't believe that it was the style, even though Sir Arthur Conan Doyle's writing skills were on par with the best thriller authors. What I found intriguing was Sherlock Holmes persona, and his way of explaining and understanding everything from (almost) nothing. A regular (even though Holmes never would say "regular") cane could reveal an entire life story.

By looking at the microcosm, as Holmes, and deconstructing everyday events until they are divided into the smallest possible parts, we can achieve new insights. The world becomes more complex than we first imagined; life a little bit more exciting ... and the brain suddenly changes.

In the context of televised football games, there is usually a group of people who before, during halftime, and after the game will try to help us viewers reach a new level of insight: we should simply understand the world of football a little bit better after their swift analysis of the game. This group of people is called "experts" because of their (potential) ability to identify (in a Holmesian way) even the tiniest of events that we simple mortals can't see or understand and then make sense of them in terms of the whole game or even the whole sport. At least, that should be the job description of an "expert."

Unfortunately we are often disappointed in the experts; well, not even disappointed, rather apathetic, as we year after year put up with their analyses – and realize that they don't take the viewer seriously. The experts should know that it's hard to fool a football fan – we are more well read than most other groups of people; we are harder to surprise. That should be an incentive for the experts to be really careful with their preparation before a game, to ponder fresh and alternative ways of articulating what is going on in the field. In the same way as a US president, the experts mostly use idiomatic expressions and metaphors that basically say nothing. Their words are vague, open for any interpretation, that is to say, they are platitudes: bland platitudes. We are thus told that "the ball is round" (in case someone missed that), "anything can happen in football" (which is probably not entirely true), and "they gave 110%" (of what?) – and this is repeated week after week by the experts, and even worse, by some of the players.

Therefore, it is no wonder that you become excited when you listen to a person who goes beyond the typical, repetitive boredom of the generic soccer studios around the world. We know that the football world is more complex than it is often portrayed in the media, so we immediately recognize an expert who can offer the new insights that we have really longed for, who takes the TV audience seriously. His name is Gary Neville (and he hates Scousers, even though he now associates with them in the studio). Strongly disliked by the audience during his playing days, Neville was embraced by the same lot when he switched professions to become an expert on Sky Sports.

To be honest, and honesty is not always that stupid, I was definitely one of those who strongly disliked the Manchester United's permanent right back as a player – how could I not? I mean: I am a Arsenal supporter, so it was obviously a traumatic and agitating experience to see Gary Neville kick down MY players (perhaps especially Jose Antonio Reyes) year after year, decade after decade. With a play style a bit like Branislav Ivanovic (worse in the offensive, but better in the defensive, and slightly more cynical), he terrorized Premier League left-wingers for nearly 20 years like a starving Rottweiler. It was never beautiful, unless your definition of 'beautiful' entails 'nasty' and 'efficient.'

But it's actually unimportant whether Gary Neville was a gracious player or not. I can hate the player but still love what he says. There is no paradox in that. So, when Gary Neville, after he put his shoes on the shelf in February 2011, made his debut as an expert on Sky Sports in the 2011/2012 season, there was no prejudice or negative anticipation, at least not from my side. And despite the fact that Manchester City had bought Sergio Aguero and Chelsea Juan Mata (and Arsenal's Carl Jenkinson) during the transfer window, it was clear after just a month that it was Sky Sports who had pulled off the recruitment of the season – the almost perfect expert was born.

For the prospective writer, it might be a good idea to read at least a couple of books by Henry Miller and Leo Tolstoy; for the aspiring comedian, it should be required to watch at least a number of appearances by Louis CK and Rory Scovel. The first question that a newly appointed expert in a football studio should ask himself is: What can I learn from Gary Neville? Sure, he has a playing career that makes it easier for him, so he can make references to his previous life on the pitch. But experience alone does not make it – his far less exciting competitor at BBC, Alan Shearer, has loads of experience as well. Yes, Neville is honest, with a brutality that equals the physicality he inflicted upon his Premier League adversaries. But Alan Hansen is also brutally honest.

What hooks my brain when Gary Neville says something has to do with his passion for details. In the summer of 2013, there were rumors that Luis Suarez would go to Arsenal, and Gareth Bale to Real Madrid (where he also went). Gary Neville gave his view of that transfer window:

> There are things in life which I would classify as noise. And noise is an irrelevance to me. Like the transfer window. I concentrate on the detail. I'm more interested in the detail of who is playing which system, or who is playing well. How does he receive the ball? Should he be in a different position? The detail of football, for me, drowns out the noise.

To listen to Gary Neville is like listening to a standup comedian. When I hear a really good standup comedian, let's say Colin Quinn, I know he has really dived into a topic, quarreled and flipped it over a few hundred times, and then articulated it in a whole new way. Colin Quinn knows that the audience will not laugh if he says the obvious: to get the audience to laugh, there must be an element of surprise, a Luis Suarez factor. The same goes for Gary Neville. If he says things that we all see on the television screen, which unfortunately too many other experts do, then the whole point of experts is superfluous. But he doesn't. That's the beauty.

He instead tell us about the problem, but also the advantage, with a South American-trained center backs position play; why Cristiano Ronaldo led him to re-evaluate what a winger should do; his pragmatic approach to diving, etc. He usually goes against the general trend of thought: he breaks down clichés, and I'm there all the way; my focus is not on any other man in the world at the moment he speaks. More than any spiritual leader, Mr. Neville allows me to be in the present.

Billy Connolly, the Scottish comedian, said in an interview that good artists can take the viewer to a place in their brains where they have never been:

> When people are really good at something – whether it's a good comedian, guitarist, sitar player, someone doing sonatas on the piano – they bring this atmosphere with them that makes you think great. You find yourself wandering off in your brain. Sensually, it wakens you up.

In the same way, I think Gary Neville affects our intellect, and I hope that he starts a revolution, that he raises the quality of all experts around the world, in much the same way that Alexis Sanchez, upon his arrival to Arsenal, forced his teammates to rise a notch or two. Then we could get a football audience with greater insights into the world of football, and thus more qualitative conversations about the sport. For now I'm content with the few minutes I get every week from Gary. In the long run, I want more. More people with passion for details. More minds like Gary Neville.

3 Say "yes."

The first time I saw Andy Cole and Dwight Yorke together, I was certain that I had witnessed something special. I had before that, of course, seen players sync with each other at a high level, like Ruud Gullit/Marco van Basten, Franco Baresi/Alessandro Costacurta, Alan Shearer/Chris Sutton, and so on and so forth. But it was still incomparable to the almost extraterrestrial communication that occurred in Manchester United's attack in the late 90's, when footballers' answer to the Sedin-twins (a perfect reference for an ice-hockey-indoctrinated Swede, less perfect for everyone else) harassed defense after defense.

Can I, before we go deeper into my thoughts about sync, tell you that I love this topic? For there is something extremely interesting in sharing a world with another person, if only for a moment.

Philosophers throughout time (perhaps mainly Immanuel Kant and his heir, Arthur Schopenhauer) have been thinking about how much we can know about the external world, about other people, and how well we can understand how another creature will react in different situations. One can imagine that the longer we live with someone, the easier it is for us to be in sync with them, but sometimes we don't even need that time because things click right away; this can happen at a new job, on a date, at a party. Or on a football field. You meet that person who invites you to dance, and you notice the ease of just being yourself, the lack of friction, how little you need to force yourself to do something. Everything just happens naturally, as in the case of Yorke/Cole.

When Cole was asked how it felt the first time he and Yorke played together, he replied, "When we first played together it was like meeting a special woman and falling in love. It felt right straight away. No matter what he did, I did the opposite. Everything worked perfectly."

Andy Cole and Dwight Yorke had, and still have, two completely different personalities. While Yorke (called The Smiling Assassin because of his constant smile) loved all the attention that he received, the more shy Cole operated in humble silence. An extrovert and an introvert, who had some sort of yin and yang relationship going on. People began to seriously wonder if there was a hidden genetic link between them. Unfortunately, the partnership of Yorke/Cole didn't last as long as we all hoped, and many thought that this was due to satiety after the amazing treble season of 98/99, something to which Cole also hinted in an interview: "Dwight is from a small Caribbean island, and I've Caribbean origin. I know about the mentality – when you reach the top, you relax and ease off. What more could Dwight do? He had already won the treble."

Anyway, for about three seasons they were the most N'sync duo we've ever seen, and therefore they were also probably one of the best attacking pairs we will ever see. And their combination goal against Barcelona at Nou Camp in the fall of 1998 was perhaps one of the most brilliant goals we've ever seen. Pure perfection.

My own experience of sync in the world of sports is incredibly strong. Let me go back to my childhood: the good old 90s, a time when I still felt that floorball (a perfect sport for a Swede, less perfect for everyone else) was a quite interesting sport; it felt fresh and new. In addition, my best friend Jonas Westlund was on my team, and together we were (at least sometimes) a fierce duo. We understood each other on a higher (or deeper) level. I also realized, even then, that there was something immensely satisfying when I saw the field in the same way as another person, to know that Jonas went for the overlap when I elegantly dropped the ball behind my back.

In football, it was definitely tougher. My idols were Michael Laudrup, Redondo, and Dennis Bergkamp, but my teammates at a young age often seemed to have a greater predilection for somewhat one-dimensional players like Romario and Jürgen Klinsmann. There were situations where I made a great through ball à la Laudrup, but unfortunately no one really saw the grandeur of the pass, and therefore no one ran on it, and there I stood with a sense of humiliation. A tough period in my life. It was not until my university years that I found a playmate who finally was in the same universe of thought: Joakim Lindberg, a great football player, and an even better friend. During a few years or so we dominated (according to us) matches in the student series, and my sense of how important it is to sync was strengthened. Football was fun again.

For isn't it something special when our brains merge with someone else's? When we are in total harmony? When we say "yes" to everything the other person does, and we know that he or she will do the same for us? I think it is something that lies deep in our nature. To have someone who makes us feel less alone in a world that can often make us feel alienated and isolated.

In today's football world, we can sometimes see traces of Yorke/Cole collaborations: Santi Cazorla and Mesut Ozil are always exciting together; Bastian Schweinsteiger and Javi Martinez were something very special in the 2012/2013 season; so were Mario Götze and Marco Reus that same season; and of course the Barca duo, Andres Iniesta and Xavi, over the last decade. But no matter how I twist and turn it, no duo had the same bond as Yorke and Cole. That gorgeous (and possibly underrated) pair that for a few years created things that, to the untrained eye, could be mistaken for magic. But it was never about magic; it was wonderfully real. It was about two people whose individual visions of football were expanded when they were together; who created something they never alone could have created; who always said "yes" to each other.

4 A strange journey.

[Published on Fotbollskanalen.se March 23, 2011]

Near the border of Canada (only 1.5 hours by car, if you drive like a maniac who has just stolen a car from another maniac), we find the hometown of Grunge Rock. Nirvana, Pearl Jam, and Soundgarden are just some of the bands that started their careers in a dark and trashy garage somewhere in Seattle. In addition to being a town for geeky musicians, Seattle is also, to a large extent, dependent on coffee. In 1971, a man named Howard Schultz got the idea to start an Italian coffee shop in Seattle. Nothing strange about that, but this café boasted unusually good profits, and so he started a few more. It was called Starbucks. Since then, coffee has been a natural part of the Emerald City. And what about football? Hm, if I put it like this, the sport that we (almost) all love hasn't been as natural a part of life in this affluent city as Starbucks. For example, it required an Internet poll in 2008 for the Seattle Sounders to be voted into the MLS, the American Premier League. But now they are here: fit, healthy, and hungry for success. The rumors also say that their audience is the biggest and the best in the league. And as Swedes, we have a few connections to this team. When the Sounders played their first match in the league in 2009, they had a Calvin Klein model in their squad, the flamboyant Freddie Ljungberg. Two years later there was another, perhaps slightly less exotic, Swede on the team: the old Häcken player, Erik Friberg, with his beautiful long hair.

Someone who has played with both of them is Osvaldo Alonso, our protagonist in this portrait, the defensive midfielder who during his debut year in the club was one of the league's most valuable players, and today is one of the first names that the German coach Sigi Schmid scribbles down when he's determining the starting eleven for the next match. But it isn't Alonso's time at the club that is the most interesting thing to talk about. Rather, it is how he managed to get to Seattle.

To understand the difficulty of his journey, it would be a good idea to mention that Alonso is from Cuba. Fidel Castro's Cuba (as you might call it, even though Fidel isn't, officially, the nation's leader anymore) is the largest country in the Caribbean; so close to the USA, yet so far away. There they make cigars that are world famous, and there they play music that is exactly as comfortable and relaxing as you want music to be. And they dance. Mambo, rumba, cha-cha-cha, some sexy salsa, you name it.

Cuba is also one of the poorest countries in the world. Confined and ostracized, both by internal politics and US trade embargos. Fidel's policy has always limited the freedom of its people, and freedom is something people need. Living in Cuba is like living in a fairly large prison, and here, in a country without hope (or at least limited hope), Osvaldo Alonso was born; in the city of San Cristobal, a town of 80,000 inhabitants on the Cuban west coast, not too far from the capital, Havana.

During the latter part of the 90st was music you thought about when Cuba was mentioned. Buena Vista Social Club, the band with the same name as the old club, had set Cuban music on the world map, and they proved that music could make you rich and successful. But Alonso liked football – and he was good at football. As a twenty-year-old boy, he received a contract from FC Pinar del Rio, a club in the Cuban top league, and from the center, he led the team to the league championship in 2006. At that time he was one of the best players in the country.

Now one can imagine what Alonso thought: "I'm one of the best in the country. I'm captain of the U-23 national team, ergo: I think I'm worthy of having my dream fulfilled, my dream of making money on this." To make money from football is one of those things you don't do in Cuba, and moving to another country was something that the President at that time, Fidel Castro, didn't appreciate. Alonso knew that: "Going on vacation; or to visit another country; or to come and go as you like ... it's not directly allowed in Cuba." Alonso's only option to achieve his dream was to escape from Cuba. How it happened, I'll tell you below.

One summer day in 2007, the Cuban national team visited Wal-Mart in Houston, Texas. The team was in the CONCACAF Gold Cup and had the day off, which meant a shopping spree focused on cheap American stuff of questionable quality. Wal-Mart was clearly the best option. Once they got inside the store, the squad began to dissolve. One can imagine that some went and looked for cheap digital cameras, some checked on those 7–8 dollar hoodies, and the rest were perhaps searching for cookies. Who knows? But one person that didn't focus on all this materialistic stuff was Osvaldo Alonso. He was nervous, and he tried to make sure that nobody was following him. Because he had a plan. An abusive regime would not burn his dreams into ashes. He would escape: "There was a lot of nervous energy. I thought about my family and whether the flight was going to be successful. I had to act quickly."

With determined steps, he headed towards the exit; it was important not to hesitate. Once he was outside the door, he didn't really know what to do – his plan didn't extend that far. But he had to move away from the store because soon his teammates would find out that he was gone. A short distance away from the store, with his heart still pumping, he managed to get hold of a Hispanic person from whom he could borrow a cell phone. He then rang a friend who lived in Miami, and after about one minute of intense conversation, it was decided: Alonso was welcome to stay at his friend's home in Miami. He quickly jumped on a bus destined for Florida.

So that was the famous day when Osvaldo Alonso made his personal escape from his samba-infested Alcatraz. And if we take a lightning-fast sidetrack, we have time to tell you a romantic story that can be connected to the Wal-Mart escape. In Cuba, years before the CONCAF Cup, a young Alonso had met a beautiful lady named Liang Perez, with whom he had fallen in love. But all is not so simple in the world of love. Being in love is not enough; it does not make everything suddenly perfect. Perez had in fact traveled to the United States while Alonso remained in Cuba.

When Alonso was asked if his love for Perez was one of the causes of his flight, he admitted: "Yes, to some extent..." Today, he is married to Perez, and together they have a son, Dennis. I mean, it's semi-beautiful, isn't it?

But back to football. Once in the USA, Alonso eventually got a contract with Charleston Battery. He was elected as the second league's (USL-1) most valuable player during his only season in Charleston after scoring seven times from his midfield position. Now he was in a lovely position to move to a bigger club, and a couple of people from Seattle did everything they could to get Alonso to the hard-working club up north. They succeeded. So here we are: at the beginning of the third season of Alonso's adventures in Seattle, the city where football will always be in the shadow of music and Starbucks. But Alonso doesn't care. Aside from freezing from time to time during the winter, the life of Osvaldo Alonso is pretty good. His dream is fulfilled – he lives well doing what he loves. And it's all thanks to some critical moments on that nervous but special day at Wal-Mart.

5 Aaron Ramsey can't fool me.

I remember a pretty interesting phone conversation with my cousin Kalle a couple of years ago. At that time we had a podcast about English football (Varför skjuter Downing?), which meant that our conversation often steered toward that subject. On this particular day, it didn't take long before we touched upon the strange case of Aaron Ramsey and his peak performance during the fall of 2013.

Statistics (which everyone became obsessed with after the book *Moneyball* was released in 2004) can clearly aid in assessing a player's performance, and statistics were definitely fun reading for Ramsey during this period. He ran most during games, he scored more goals than anyone else, and he won more tackles than he ever had before. No matter what you read about Ramsey, it was positive: positive words and positive numbers. It felt almost surreal.

A year earlier, one thing that united Arsenal fans was the opinion that the more imminent Ramsey's departure from the club, the better. So perhaps it was this feeling that was circulating in my body when I confessed to Kalle that I was still worried when I saw Ramsey's name in the starting lineup. I had a feeling that his frequent bloopers from the year before were still part of the young midfielder's standard repertoire; that statistics now played tricks with our minds; that we all felt some kind of false security when Ramsey got the ball.

To draw an interesting parallel to Ramsey, we can go back a couple of years to when the tricky Belarusian, Aleksander Hleb, played for Arsenal. Here was a man whose skills didn't translate well into numbers. Few assists, even fewer goals, and sometimes limited movement on the field – a disaster if you only looked at the statistics. But, and this is a big BUT, another interpretation could be: (a) a player who probably had the most "third assists" (or hockey assists) in the league, and (b) a player that moved cleverly rather than far – a player who was an expert at moving and passing between the opposing lines, which opened up unique opportunities for his teammates.

But how often will these elements be part of a statistical analysis? How can you incorporate these factors into numbers?

Talk show host Conan O'Brien, known for his fluffy red hair, spoke in an interview about his skeptical attitude toward the analysis of comedy:

> I'm very careful about analyzing comedy. Being a comedian is like being a chef: You take a little salt, a little oregano, and throw in a piece of this and that. You don't measure anything, and don't try to follow any chemical formula.

To take Conan's thought a step further: Maybe it's a deeper criticism I would like to express here, a critique of quantitative science? Maybe I have listened to too many sermons about why we should stop smoking (I haven't succeeded) and how everything these days is about growth in our world. Too many narrow-minded analyses of slices and garnishes, too few thoughts and reflections on the whole pie.

I'm worried that we get stuck in using statistics as our only tool to understand football; that it determines how we look at each individual performance; that we forget how complex the world is, and by extension how complex every footballer is; that the language of statistics thrives on simplicity and obscures complexity.

But I don't think I am the only one who walks around and thinks about this every now and then. Nassim Nicholas Taleb, who wrote the book *Antifragile*, where he discusses this topic among other things, writes, "Life is more, much more, labyrinthine than our memory shows – our brain tries to transform history into something smooth and linear, which make us underestimate the complexity of life." Taleb would probably smile pleasantly at me if I communicated my thoughts to him. And Conan O'Brien also seems to be in tune with the same kind of thinking beneath that fluffy red hair. And, in the end, maybe even my (also redhead) cousin, who at the end of our phone conversation said, "Oscar, I'm not stupid, I know what's going on...maybe Ramsey can fool average Joe...but he can't fool me."

6 Hypothetically.

A medical researcher (and football geek) at Umeå University in northern Sweden has created a pill that makes you void of any "negative" emotions while watching a football game. The pill also has the power to smooth your mood if your favorite team loses, i.e., you will not behave like an asshole towards your partner hours after the game. No study has been done on the long-term consequences, but the ingredients in the pill are not dangerous, and the short-term consequences are obviously positive. Would you take the pill? If not: Why?

7 Press and stress.

I used to think my brain was deadly quick; I thought I reacted to situations with the speed of a cobra. But in retrospect, I have begun to doubt whether that was something positive. For it's one thing to respond quickly, and quite another to make accurate decisions (which I didn't). I was more like George Costanza in Seinfeld – my poorly developed instincts led me wrong.

This was particularly evident on the football field. A young Oscar Oberg was a fully capable player, even gifted, some would say, assuming I had the chance to dictate the game at my own, often too pleasant, pace. But there was one thing I really hated: when opponents pressed high. It was terrifying. In this way, I was also very fragile.

I particularly remember one time at Vildmannavallen (our home ground) in Umeå, maybe 2001 or 2002. From kickoff, a teammate passed the ball backwards (probably Johan Eriksson, who was often entrusted as a center forward in our pretty weak offensive line), and as a center back, I was hoping to in a calm manner make a neat pass to prove to the crowd (of ten people) that they were watching a future Swedish international. But no. From nowhere, two opponents (I think Rundvik was our opponent...) came at ridiculously high speed towards me, which increased my heart rate by approximately 700% and caused a sort of panic state in me that only people in war and football can understand. A few seconds later, Rundvik had taken the lead. What happened is that, showing an amazing lack of logic, I had tried to dribble, but the uneven ground of Vildmannavallen fooled me. I slipped. And they took the ball. And they scored.

The French philosopher Jean-Jacques Rousseau wrote in his autobiography *Confessions*:

> To think, I must be coldblooded. I make excellent impromptu when I first must think things over in peace and quiet, but in the heat of the moment I have never done or said anything that is good enough.

This reasoning, I think, fits me perfectly, and I have a feeling that a great majority of the world's footballers think the same. We humans do and say strange things when our heart rate goes up; it's like our brain, suddenly, is disconnected. Our heart rate goes up because we come across something that we aren't really accustomed to, an interesting psychological phenomenon that all exciting teams from the past have exploited: the Hungarian team of the 50s, Ajax (the

70s), Dynamo Kiev (80s), Milan (90s), Barcelona (2000s), and today's Bayern Munich. They have understood the deeper meaning of high and intense pressure, of never giving the opponents the chance to analyze beyond their immediate instincts.

Each team has a kind of collective consciousness, that is, if a teammate is stressed, it is hard to not be affected yourself. It is therefore sufficient for a team with high press to instill panic in a couple of opponents to create fear in an entire team. In theory, most football players know how to react to high press, they are even carefully trained to handle it, but in reality nobody always reacts as they should in theory (the author Daniel Kahneman, who wrote the book *Thinking, Fast and Slow* probably has formulated all this in a more intelligent way...).

I'm just saying I am happy that I am not involved in football today: it doesn't fit my relatively low-energy style of play. Teams like Jürgen Klopp's Liverpool, Pep Guardiola's Bayern Munich, and all the teams that Marcelo Bielsa is in charge of make me tired feel just looking at them: it's like all those teams are on some superdrug, or have two hearts, or both.

High press made me slip. But it is perhaps also why I think it's interesting to watch these high press teams. I want to see events that can't be predicted; I want to see strange reactions: when the brain shuts down, and instincts take over; when control of the future disappears, and people react more like a confused and frustrated George Costanza. In those moments football is captivating. In those times, football is fun.

Don't pressure me to write anymore now because I have to finish this before I feel too much stress about the fact that I haven't showered before my friend's birthday party tonight. Peace.

8 Fantasy Premier League.

I have always loved fantasy worlds. It started with JRR Tolkien's Lord of the Rings trilogy, continued with the PG Wodehouse's utopian world, and then with all literature that made me wander to more exciting places than Umeå. Maybe it's some kind of escapism from a cold and hard reality, but I'm not going to do a Freudian analysis on myself and dig deeper into that. To make it simple: it's just fun to occasionally live in a fantasy.

So, it wasn't unexpected that I jumped at the chance to join Fantasy Premier League 8 years ago. FPL (as I will call it in the future) is a free online game where participants choose an imaginary squad consisting of two goalkeepers, five defenders, five midfielders, and three attackers, with a budget of £ 100 million, which can then increase or decrease depending on whether the players' value goes up or down. Before each round, you select eleven players from your squad (and a team captain), and you then receive points (double points for the team captain) for them based on how they performed on the field, i.e., if your players have scored, made assists, kept clean sheets, or received any magical bonus points (calculated by the sports company Opta).

Without digging into all the rules, it should be mentioned that the game is so dynamic that if you forget to change formations for two weeks, there is a real chance that you have spoiled all your hope of a reasonably good finishing position when the season concludes in May. It is a harsh climate, but for those who make the effort the reward is pretty awesome. You can get top 4 in your league. Or go to the fifth round of the Cup. Both epic achievements.

Let's look a little bit at the history of the game: It grew popular sometime in the mid 90s, and since then FPL has only grown in popularity – right now more than 3 million frustrated geeks try to put together their ultimate squads each season. And of the three million, there are also a lot of so-called "celebrities" who realized that this game is more than just a game – it's a lifestyle (first exaggeration – there will be more). Last year, the British tennis star Andy Murray mentioned that, "I have won my league 2 out of 3 times, and I plan to win again this year. We also have a trophy awarded each year with the winner's name on it; right now it stands in my trophy cabinet, in front of all my tennis trophies." When asked whether it even stood in front of his Olympic gold medal, he replied with a short and distinct, "Yes."

And speaking of British people, when Tony Blair was Prime Minister of UK, he let teachers know that Fantasy football was a good tool to help young people learn math: "Fantasy Football is perhaps imagination, but the math is real. Dealing with the weak math results we have had recently is one of our priorities right now. To incorporate something that young people can relate to we believe can make a big difference." Tony Blair clearly saw, which too few have given him credit for, the relationship between FPL and genius kids.

But even people from other parts of the world see the greatness in FPL. Prince Abdullah of Saudi Arabia once called George Gillett, Liverpool's former partner, to get some inside info on Steven Gerrard:

> I remember that I once called George Gillett, the owner of Liverpool – I wanted to know if Steven Gerrard would play that weekend's game, because I had him on my fantasy team. I said, "Can you find out if Gerrard will play?" He said he would do his best. I often try to find out what happens. I have many friends who give me information about the players and hopefully I will have access to even more information in the future.

You understand? This is important. But there is a small problem that you might already have figured out... and that's when Premier League players themselves create teams, something that is already happening, and which blurs the line between fantasy and reality.

In January 2013, it was revealed that large parts of the Stoke City team had their own FPL league. The leader of the league was Peter Crouch with his team Longpins Longballers, followed closely by Ryan Shotton's FC Shottinho and Jamie Ness's Nessinators. The interesting thing about Peter Crouch's team was that he had selected himself until he realized that he was in a slump – he then swapped to Demba Ba, a transfer that either demonstrated bad self-confidence or extraordinary self-awareness.

The same year, during the autumn, it also was revealed that Leon Osman was a confirmed FPL player when his teammate Leighton Baines, after a win against West Ham where he made two goals, told the interviewer: "Ossie [Osman] had taken me out of his fantasy football because I was not producing enough amount of points, so I told him I would make some goals. I kept my word."

But it gets stranger. West Bromvich goalkeeper Ben Foster was faced with a difficult choice when his team was up against Manchester United, which at the time had the most popular of all FPL players: Robin van Persie, a player that Foster himself had on his FPL team. So that there wouldn't be an uncomfortable situation, Foster told the *Sun* that he had to replace Van Persie: a loss for his FPL team, but probably a must in order to not be split in order to prevent split interests in his "real" life.

Is there a conflict of interest in the above examples? Yes, definitely. Do you still think it is possible to justify the fact that Premier League players participate in FPL? Yes, definitely. Some would compare FPL with betting, which in that case would be prohibited because players aren't allowed to bet under the FA's rules. However, there is a difference: first, players don't compete for any visible money. But above all, FPL is so much more fun than betting. It would be awful to prohibit the Premier

League players this unique opportunity to bring happiness into their lives.

So, how does your team produce, Oscar? My team, Stekiga Renen FC, with the Darth Vader-inspired all-black outfit that I have tried to popularize, has been a successful team in many ways. Sure, I had a dip in 2009/2010, when I only finished 1,917,421, but it was because I gave up after seven games when I noticed that my Chelsea-hating strategy didn't work out. Otherwise, Stekiga Renen FC has delivered. The peak came in the 2012/2013 season, when I managed to sneak into place 14,517, which was a feat comparable to sailing around the world in an e-dinghy.

In Sweden, we have this forum called Flashback where people (usually trolls) can write about anything, and of course Flashback has its own thread about Fantasy Football. Since I'm in Flashback's own league, I show up in this thread on the forum occasionally to see how my teammates feel. From time to time, I look at this thread, and I see some interesting patterns in the conversations:

A) The most common comment is one expressing disappointment for a useless game week.

Example: "Damn what a bad week for me ended at 38p ☹"

This is expected because most people who play this game live in an illusion. We think we can somehow play god and control the output of each gameweek, and thus get 100p week after week. When we discover that Wayne Rooney once again let us down, we are obviously upset, which we like to point out to the other forum members.

B) Anxiety before every game seems to be virtually mandatory.

Example: "Have anxiety before the gameweek. My team: Boruc-Jagielka, Coleman, Hangeland-Lallana, Yaya, Ramsey, Ozil-Aguero, Costa, Giroud. Subs: Olsson, Whittaker, and Albrighton. Almost all players face one another, looking to throw in Olsson instead of

Jagielka and just take a shit-round and then save my change to next week. Any suggestions?"

Example 2: "Have a hard time to make a decision, hope some clever person can help me: Have had a pretty shaky start in the FPL with a lot of injuries and such, but now the squad is as good as healthy (except Silva), but needs help!"

These two examples clearly show how important it is to find the right starting lineup before the gameweek begins – with the wrong formation, the disappointment will be great, as in example A. To minimize the chance of making a fool of yourself, it might be good to follow Prince Abdullah's advice, i.e., to do thorough research regarding injuries and trends and have an eye on the game schedule (both short- and long-term) so you don't end up with three players that have an away game against Manchester City.

C) Who will wear the captain's armband (the C) is also a frequent topic of discussion.

Example: "For the third week in a row my captain underperformed... Nasri this week, Benteke last week, and Hazard the week before..."

Answer to the previous example: "Bumbibeer, you're not alone. Sturridge naturally managed to stay away from all four goals for Liverpool. It is the third week in a row that my captain only made 2 points. Amazing..."

The captain's points are counted twice. Now you understand why it hurts when you fail in your choice of captain. Life feels heavy. But when you see Giroud score a hat trick and you know that there is a (C) under his name in the lineup, all the previous pain is outweighed by the sheer joy. Life feels like a gift once again.

D) Finally, there are also those who want to tell you what an amazing team they have.

Example: "I feel pretty happy with the team I have. Mignolet-Bertrand, Fonte, Hangeland-Ayew, Payet, Ozil, Sanchez-Vardy, Giroud, Ighalo. Subs: Fabianski, Richards, Mahrez, Hutton. Feels like good players that all can bring me some points. Saints face Leicester home the next round, a good chance for two of my defenders to keep a clean sheet. And I also expect my Arsenal trio to keep getting points. I mean, I don't see how they wouldn't against Watford."

To brag about your team is little bit un-Swedish – but I fully understand those who do. I have to admit, I'm also guilty of this sin (or virtue). There is something beautiful in telling the world that you have solved all the mysteries: you have formed the perfect set-up based on the scarce resources you began with. You feel like Gandalf sitting with all the answers; you've found the bug that everyone is looking for.

But let's not go into more examples now – it's time to draw some sort of conclusion about this fantasy world. Listen: You know those things in life that are really fun when you make them, but afterwards you feel they were kind of unnecessary because they didn't generate any value for your future? To sit for an hour (or two... or four) in front of the FPL and ponder the lineup when you used the wildcard provides exactly that feeling. But I'm not sure I want to abandon this activity because there is almost nothing better than achieving a total score of 100 points while finding out from a phone call that your friend only managed a sad 27 points. Suddenly, your full time job as an FPL player is worth it.

And somehow I think that all this fantasizing is good for us, because this is a game that benefits the player with good knowledge of human nature – those at the top have a clear sense of how teams and players are feeling at the moment, and they can thus, to some extent, predict the future. Therefore, the more you truly understand other people, the better you perform in FPL. So, and this may be far-fetched (it is probably far-fetched), I imagine that FPL not only makes us better mathematicians, as Tony Blair said earlier, but ultimately turns us into more understanding and better people... huh? You heard me! I stand by my (admittedly somewhat shaky) final theory and now leave this story to go check on my lineup.

9 In the footsteps of Simone de Beauvoir.

Recently, after some conversations with my mother, I came to think about identity: who we are, and what forces influence us to become who we are. Of course, my irreparably damaged brain immediately tried to connect these thoughts to football.

The philosopher Alan Watts, who has been one of the best translators of eastern philosophical ideas to the western world, wrote about how socially conditioned we all are in his short but thoughtful book, *The Book on the Taboo Against Knowing Who You Are*:

> We seldom realize, for example, that our most private thoughts and emotions are not actually our own. For we think in terms of language and images which we didn't invent, but which were given to us by our society. We copy emotional reactions from our parents, learning from them that excrement is supposed to have a disgusting smell and that vomiting is supposed to be an

> unpleasant sensation. The dread of death is also learned from their anxieties about sickness and from their attitude to funerals and corpses.

Similarly, a football player is born into the language of football. In youth, we learn that there are left backs and right backs, defensive midfielders and offensive midfielders, goalkeepers and strikers, all with clear role descriptions. We are taught that a match is played over a limited period, with rules that govern our play and conduct. We are taught that it's about winning (and that it is usually Jose Mourinho who wins).

All this is hardly natural (even though the term "natural" is also up for discussion). The message that "the most important thing is to win" is no original thought that Mother Earth has given us; football rules are not direct commandments from God; and we are not born a left back, it's something we become (as Simone de Beauvoir would have expressed it if she had been interested in the world's most beautiful sport).

For most people that are introduced to the world of football, there are preprinted scripts for how to behave, scripts that are so established that they can get you trapped in their language and view of the world. Dennis Bergkamp talks in his book *Stillness and Speed* about how this script has only gotten stronger over the years in his parent club Ajax:

> If you look at the coaches we have now, they're so different. They all have their badges, and they are all very sympathetic and know exactly how to play football and what kind of exercises you should do, and for how many minutes, and the distances between the goals, and where the cones should be where you're playing positional games. And they know not to play too long – one and a half hours maximum. They all know exactly how everything should be done. Maybe that's the problem. We never had that sort of attention, so we were more self-taught.

It is in this "exact" environment that most football players are brought up. I have a feeling that few coaches ask their players to critically examine football concepts and language, and that few coaches even want their players to do so because it might cause confusion, give rise to discussions, and ultimately undermine the clear hierarchy that exists in most football clubs.

But I think it can be of great interest for a footballer to ask basic questions, like the Japanese engineers who always ask "why?" six times in order to get to the bottom of the problem. What is football? What does it mean to live in this sometimes strange world of football? What values are almost forced upon me by the coaches? What is my proper place on the field? Must I forever be locked into a position, a label some coach I vaguely remember once gave me when I was a teenager? Are there rules on the field and within the club that I think are unnecessary? Do I dare violate them? What makes me happiest when I'm on a football field? Is it really most important for me to win, or is there something about the process itself that is of greater importance? What can I do to express myself as freely as possible, both verbally and physically, without hurting someone else? And why don't I have long and beautiful dreadlocks like Derek Boateng?

These questions may not always lead to greater success on the football field, but they can lead to greater self-awareness, and ultimately, increased freedom: a sense of being something more than "just" a football player who obeys orders; a liberation from the intellectual prison that you have lived in since that first organized training when you were 7 years old and your coach said, "You will play left back."

As a writer, I'm socially conditioned to have a conclusion at the end of a text, but I think Alan Watts would be proud of me if I just finish here.

10 Minimalism.

[*Published in GOAL number 10/2011*]

Back in the days when I went to preschool in my hometown of Umeå, we often had football players from the leading football club in town, Umeå FC, as teachers. It was cool (or at least a little bit). And when they played with us during the breaks, I was fascinated because without moving much they still dominated the matches. They looked like magicians, but they were really something completely different: they were minimalists. They knew the principles needed to own a bunch of 7 year old maniacs with limited understanding of the game: they just took a small touch here and there, stood in perfect position on defense, and made ugly but invisible pullings when a quick Oscar Oberg was coming through.

With age I also became a football minimalist. From being a super energetic (well, maybe not super – let's say energetic...) dribbler à la Michael Laudrup when I was 9 or 10 years old, I became more and more selective with my own running with each passing year, and I started to become very fond of the center circle: I was drawn to it, like Gollum was drawn to the one ring. I realized that the more I passed the ball, the less I needed to run. Brilliant. Others looked enviously at my shirt, which after the match was as fresh as when I had started. I had, according to myself, found a beautiful shortcut to greatness. And, unlike Gollum, I got away with it.

It has therefore been easy for me to connect with football players who don't move around like crazy greyhounds: Those who, with limited resources and great tactical ability, set the pace for the team. The conductors. I will now present my first minimalist love: Fernando Redondo, the player who with stillness and speed never made things more difficult than they needed to be. It looked so simple when Redondo floated around on the field, but playing simple is often more difficult than you think. With mediocre technique it is a major challenge; with a big ego, it is impossible.

Most South American stars come from, by Swedish standards, poor conditions and humble circumstances. Not Redondo – he comes from a wealthy family, where tender beef on the dining table was an everyday reality rather than a dream. He didn't have to become a professional football player, but a professional football player he became. In 1985, a 16-year-old Redondo made his debut for Argentino Juniors, the club that had previously been represented by Diego Maradona (and later came to nurture Juan Roman Riquelme). Redondo's technique was extraordinary, and the club management wanted him to play as a number 10, but Redondo himself liked to be a little further back, as a number 5, where he was able to dictate the game in peace and quiet, like a somewhat more extroverted Ferdinand the Bull.

If we fast forward the tape almost 10 years to 1994, past the time he spent in Juniors and later at Tenerife, the next stop for our hero was Real Madrid – the period that made his name go down in the history books. For more than half a decade, Redondo ruled Real's midfield with a very soft iron fist: opponents felt sick because of his tendency to always manage to cut off their best attacking options while teammates thrived in Redondo presence.

Perhaps his finest moment came against Manchester United at Old Trafford in the second quarter finals of the Champions League on April 19th, 2000. Manchester had managed to draw at the Bernabeu two weeks earlier, and as the defending champions were now clear favorites to go to the final. After about 50 minutes it was 3-0 to Real: Scholes, Giggs, Beckham, Keane, the lot of them, had at times been totally outplayed by Los Merengues, and the superbrain behind Real's "joga bonito" was Redondo. His backheel dribble past Henning Berg, which led to the 3-0 goal, was the moment when it became more than a win. It became a humiliation. After the game, Sir Alex Ferguson was confused. He wondered how Redondo could play like this, "What has this player in his shoe? A magnet?" Real won the Champions League, and El Principe (his nickname) won the prize as the most valuable player of the tournament – and a few months later, also the prize as the best player in the Spanish league in the 90s. This was the culmination of Redondo's career and the end of an era in Real's history, pre-Los Galacticos.

Redondo finished his years as a professional player in Milan from 2000 to 2004, a period in which he was less successful due to injuries and problematic relationships with authoritarian national team coaches Carlos Billardo (coach of Argentina at the 1990 World Cup) and Daniel Passarella (WC 1998). These conflicts and two missed World Cups are probably the factors that stop people from talking about Redondo as one of the biggest stars we have experienced in recent decades. But those who followed Real Madrid during that magic period between 1994 and 2000 will never forget the maestro from Buenos Aires – a complete player, a unique specimen, who usually took care of three midfield roles by himself. A perfect minimalist, who proved the beauty in simplicity.

11 St. Totteringham's Day.

It's strange. My connection to my favorite team Arsenal is extremely loose, and definitely has no geographical arguments behind it (born in Umeå and living in Stockholm). Yet I celebrate St. Totteringham's Day (the day when it is mathematical impossible for Tottenham to end before Arsenal in the table) with joy every year. First, I have to say that I don't go around hating Tottenham 24/7; it's not that I'm yearning for mishaps and misfortunes on their behalf. I clearly choose my occasions. There are mainly two (even though there are more) things I don't want to happen during the year: 1. The Spurs finish in front of Arsenal in the Premier League table. 2. The Spurs win any of the so-called North London derbies. If those things don't occur, I am satisfied, even happy – everything beyond that is a bonus (like the Spurs being in the relegation battle). However, if any of these evil things occur (the last time example 1 happened, George Graham was still a coach at Arsenal...), I will probably be in an unpleasant mood; conversations with friends/family are cut down to the verge of non-existence; an anger against society in general is built up. Above all, my anger towards anyone who in any way connected to the Spurs is extreme at this point, and my eyes when I meet any of these people are reminiscent of the eyes of Anakin Skywalker just before he goes over to the dark (best?) side. It sounds a little bit crazy. It probably is a bit crazy, but there is also something amusing, almost fun about it.

The thing is: I feel that we are all good and bad, that we have both a devil and an angel in us, but being good is not as fun as being evil. So, if we oppress our good side and let the evil come out, we can for a moment be someone that others can laugh at; we might even laugh at ourselves in retrospect. Isn't that worth something? Doesn't it create a slightly bizarre added value, a value that might be a little strange to speak of, but that is out there and disproves that hatred is always a bad thing? But regardless if I really believe in this stuff about added value, I will probably never stop hating the Spurs. It's simply just too fun. I can love all people who love the Spurs, and there are definitely times when I have been involved in group hugs with these strange people, but for a certain period I will also hate them. I think they understand (and if they don't understand, they're REALLY typical Spurs fans...). To embrace and accept all the socially non-correct emotions that appear when you support a football team, I think, is one of the roads to unlimited happiness, and if I ever write a self-help book, it will definitely be my one big theory that the rest of the book is based on.

See you next St. Totteringham's Day! Should be any day now...

12 Hypothetically.

An oil billionaire who never liked football (the rumor was that he was always chosen last when they played football in school) wants to steer the world towards becoming less football loving. He has decided to give 1 million dollars to all football geeks on the condition that they never watch a football game again. If you unknowingly come in contact with a match in any way, for example, if you go into a cafe where they show Swansea vs. Southampton on a TV screen behind the counter, you have a couple of seconds to look away, but if you consciously choose to go to an environment where it is likely you'll see Eden Hazard, let's say O'Learys or your football loving cousin's apartment at 15:00 on a Saturday, the money is gone. Do you accept the proposal? If 1 million isn't enough, is there any sum that would be acceptable?

13 Rebellion.

I've never really liked punk music, but I've always liked punk attitude. When I hear Sid Vicious bass lines, I do not feel any nice sensations in my body, but when

Johnny Rotten sings "And I Wanna be Anarchy," I understand. I understand what punk means.

Punk philosophy basically means to question everything and everyone, and in the likely case of dislike, tell them to f**ck off. To wake up from apathy. To free oneself from social norms. Features from punk philosophy can be seen in Taoism's most central text, the Tao Te Ching, but perhaps even more from famous anarchists like Pierre-Joseph Proudhon, Alexander Berkman, and Emma Goldman, and their ideas about freedom. And then punk turned the volume on these ideas "Up To Eleven," as Nigel Tufnel (far-fetched reference, I know) would have described it.

Which makes me think of Stuart Pearce. During the 80s and 90s, Pearce was pure punk on the football field: with the same crazy eyes as Black Flags singer Henry Rollins and the same energy as the Vandals. Even though his hair was extremely bland, and his name even blander, his passion was enough to earn him the nickname "Psycho." Along the left side, Pearce ran with one of the most intense glances the football world had ever seen, and that made all the world's right wingers think once or twice before they went into a challenge with the crazy left back. And I understand why: I mean, to meet a psychopath, whether it's on the football field or not, never feels particularly safe. For Pearce, punk music is said to have helped him to vent his somewhat wild nature. In an interview, he told a reporter: "When I was young, I didn't listen to slow songs or ballads. It did not fit my personality. I just wanted to listen to something fast and powerful that I could sing along to and bounce up and down on the bed at, like a complete fool."

Today, we have another punk star, Zlatan Ibrahimovic, but he is totally different in style. The one thing that connects the two is the search for adrenaline rushes. To fight against apathy. While a young Pearce got it by bouncing to punk music, Zlatan got it by stealing bikes. Where the footballer Pearce got it through tackles, Zlatan got it from bicycle kicks.

Zlatan has everything punk stands for. If reporters behave like idiots, Zlatan will let them know; if Pep Guardiola tells him not to drive his Ferrari Enzo to training, everyone knows that he will park his black sports car outside the Ciutat Esportiva Joan Gamper the next day. He says what he wants, and he does what he wants. Growing up in Rosengård was perhaps harsh in some way, but it gave Zlatan something unique: a lesson in how to be self-reliant in an environment that did not give him a helping hand. DIY (do it yourself), a phrase from the punk world, was fully integrated in Zlatan's mind at an early age.

All this makes Zlatan popular in a country like Sweden, where people usually don't deviate from the norms, and he is fully aware of the qualities that make people love him. When Zlatan was asked, "Can you explain why you are so popular?" in an interview, he replied, "Because I am honest with myself and I don't allow myself to be someone other than who I am. And I always dare to try new things."

I don't know, but the concept of freedom is such a common theme in my texts that it should be counted as an obsession – something strange must have happened in my childhood, for sure. But it's not such a bad obsession. I mean, the really inspiring figures in our history, such as Jesus, Lao-Tse, and Buddha, have always had a desire for liberation. But there are more people like that, even in our time. You can find them in punk music; in comedy; and in football, for sure. Those souls that make us hungry to live.

Yesterday gave us Stuart Pearce. This day gives us Zlatan. Who will be our lifesaving football rebel tomorrow, we do not know yet. Because we need rebellion. We need punk. We need a little bit of anarchy in our life.

14 Victoria Concordia Crescit.

I often, or at least sometimes, get the question: Why Arsenal? And then maybe some other questions like: Is there something exciting about such a choice? Why not choose something unique (like a division 3 team from Slovenia) instead? Or a team with some obscure billionaire owner from southern Italy? The problem with questions like these is that they are really too intellectual. For I am a human being (even though some I know believe they can prove otherwise), and being a human being means that my intelligence is limited: I don't always think that much when I make a choice. Many people I talk football with have these long stories that will last at least 15 minutes, an often rather boring amplification about the circumstances that made them who they are (no matter how the story begins, most still end with the words: "And that's why I love Liverpool"). My story is that my brother liked (that's right) Liverpool, and I disliked my brother's preferences, which meant that I decided to cheer on the second top team at the time (this was around 1990), namely Arsenal.

In the current situation, I am happy with my choice: Arsenal plays an interesting football, and I'm honestly excited before each match. Of course I sometimes scream when we're soft on defense, and more than sometimes I scream at Aaron Ramsey. But who doesn't? Being a bit upset is just delightful if it isn't in overly large doses. On the other hand, I am grateful that I support a team that practices the sport I love better than many others, at least from my perspective of what good football is. In my view, I get almost 90 minutes of quality time each week.

One of my favorite comedians, Pete Holmes, with one of my favorite podcasts (*You made it weird with Pete Holmes* - download it at iTunes!), said in an interview that good comedy can have a healing effect on us: "I know it's a bit pretentious to say, but I want our show to make your life better, because I believe that good comedy can make you feel better at the end of the day, or at least it should." I agree. And I not only agree: I think in the same way that good football makes me feel better, and with Arsenal odds are fairly good that my aesthetic nerve becomes satisfied.

But before I take this argument too far, let me add a few factors that could have changed my choice: a) If I had a strong local connection to any other club that would be different; b) If I'd watched more games live, because then the atmosphere in the stands would be just as interesting as the game itself; and c) If I had a bunch of friends that all loved the same club, and they had been able to influence me (I'm always falling for peer pressure, because it's fun!).

But even then, I would question myself: Is it worth it? To see a team that plays a type of football that I don't feel good about? I don't know, it's a difficult question, and that is why I am writing this text - to develop my inner thoughts. Maybe there is something deeper in the organization's roots that could get me to accept a mediocre playing style: maybe something with the club's philosophy, that their values are consistent with my own; perhaps a slight feeling of a latent potential. But even if I liked the organization's philosophy, should I torment myself with 90 minutes of misery? I don't think so. I must be frank with you. I cannot feed my soul with limitless negative sensations. Life is too short.

Victoria Concordia Crescit.

15 Tragedy, comedy, and my opportunistic brother.

I found a great quote when I, without any goal, just lazily Googled around (which I too often do). Do you want to hear? No? I'll tell it anyway, and I do it with joy:

"This world is a comedy for those who think and a tragedy for those who feel."

Why is it good? Why has the British writer Horace Walpole, who has been dead for a couple of hundred years, managed to capture my interest? Because the quote rings true. At least for me. The more I think, the easier I can see the humor in Arsène Wenger's nervousness. The more I feel, the easier I become annoyed with those who see the humor in Arsène Wenger's nervousness.

Football and love are two areas where I more often feel rather than think, where I make strange decisions and reach emotional states that I didn't know I had. This means that I suffer when I watch my Arsenal with other people who don't care as much as I do. Those who think instead of feel. Those who laugh when Per Mertesacker slips, or who mock Mikel Arteta's perfect hairstyle. Right there and then, I hate these people enormously.

I think I have come to the realization that I will always be this way: I will always be an emotional wreck when Arsenal plays. I don't know if it is always healthy, but I have a feeling that it can sometimes be useful to switch between emotions – to exploit the full emotional spectrum, which can often be severely underutilized in human beings. When the match is over, the grieving process begins, but during the game all feelings are allowed. Even crying (when Thierry Henry made his comeback for Arsenal in January 2012 and scored against Leeds in the FA Cup, tears came, totally unexpected, which I don't seem entirely comfortable telling you guys about, so therefore it pops up in these parentheses rather than in the real text).

I know how non-football people – "normal" people – look at this. They think I'm ridiculous. But I think like this: If you have children, you understand how other parents are feeling. Right? And when your child, a little bit clumsy, walks into a door and starts crying, you obviously don't laugh, even though from an intellectual viewpoint you can see the humor in the situation (and perhaps wish that you had captured the incident on video and could send it to one of these bloopers shows on TV). It works exactly the same way with football supporters. And I don't mean supporters like my brother, who once every six months watches a Liverpool match, and only discusses them when they are playing like they did in the spring of 2014. He's a non-committed dad in that way. He doesn't care about the team's development, crises, all the interesting stuff that only one who looks really carefully can see – he just wants to be part of the fun when there is fun to be part of. He isn't like many of us who have daily contact with our children, i.e., our favorite club; we who update ourselves about injuries and watch all sorts of interviews to get a better feel for the atmosphere among the players. We are the committed parents. My brother is like the goofy uncle who shows up with candy and plastic toys and celebrates with the children in a giddy sugary orgy. But after he leaves, smiling and filled with self-pride, who is left to clean up the mess and talk the kids down from their post-rush crash? (I really don't think I can stretch this analogy further now…).

How you relate to football is obviously an individual thing, and as the Buddha said: "Nothing is better or worse than the other." But I always try to explain to friends, family, and really, every person I encounter the interesting thing that happens when you truly surrender to a team, to this strange emotional roller coaster, where you let a bunch of strangers decide how you will feel in the near future. I know how that sounds; it sounds so damn irrational.

But that's also the beauty of loving a team: to decide that at least once a week to feel rather than think; not to reflect or ridicule the feelings that arise, but to just dive into the sensations that occur when Olivier Giroud receives the ball with a too heavy touch and see where they take you.

16 Hypothetically.

I love Seinfeld. A lot. Too much, could even be argued. The other day I watched the episode "The Contest" for maybe the 34th time in my life, which sounds a bit tragic, and perhaps indicates a certain inability to renew myself. But anyway: In this episode Jerry, Kramer, Elaine, and George bet who can avoid touching themselves, that is, masturbate, for the longest time. It becomes a contest in patience and willpower. To fight against extreme forces. To go against our nature.

So, imagine that players from Europe's four biggest first leagues (the English, German, Italian, and Spanish) are gathered on an island, a very beautiful island where they get access to beautiful bungalows and delicious food whenever they want. They will also be served alcohol, which of course can be fun, but for our competition can have dire consequences. Because all over the island there are also soccer balls spread out, new perfect Nike balls (no product placement, I promise) that just want to be kicked. What does this mean, you wonder? Look, most of the players have lived with a football for 15–30 years, and some for even 40. Their love of kicking a football is deeply ingrained.

The competition is: The one that lasts the longest without touching a ball wins free wishes from a holy spirit. This is huge. But during these days (or weeks, or maybe even months/years/decades) these footballers' willpower will be tested. Who do you think will win? Who will fail the fastest? And how much will the alcohol affect Artur Boruc's chances for a reasonably acceptable place in the competition?

17 In a studio with George Costanza.

I have watched football on TV a ridiculous amount of times. Really. And I have a theory: If we peel away all the layers of "show business" from a football studio, i.e., the formal Hugo Boss suits, their pretty makeup, and the sterile studio environment, I am quite sure that we could get into a dialogue that doesn't suck. Because I want to watch a studio discussion and feel "Oh, there's something interesting happening here. It is a challenging discussion, but at the same time playful. They have fun... and wait... I learn something too!"

First, isn't it crazy to put people in a studio who don't really know each other? How will they dare to stretch each other's boundaries? Are they really going to challenge each other and take the discussion a step further? In a safe environment, among friends, we can always go deep, and in great moments actually find something of value, because we know that none of what we say comes from a bad place in our heart. In an environment with strangers, I think that we sometimes put on a filter, which not only separates all evil thoughts but also separates the exciting thoughts.

And I'm not sure about presenters: Do we really need them? Isn't it a sign that we are scouting socially awkward people for TV? That we need a hostess as a social lubricant to ask the most basic questions that can be asked, and to never get a question in return? It's somehow unnatural; this is not what a good conversation in my world looks like. And let me say this: I think the reason that podcasts have become a global success is that we for the first time are able to listen to people that actually talk to each other without clearly defined roles that they must fulfill. If we can watch the magic that happens in the podcast sphere and try to cope with that vibe, I think we can also find something beautiful in a football studio.

Anyway, I also have a problem with the clothes that people are wearing in studios. For some reason, sports journalists tend to dress like bankers, in stark contrast to the sweaty, smelly, dirty players they earn their living on. I mean, have you ever seen a man in a three-piece suit and tie say something deep and insightful? In a suit, you are correct and professional, organized and polite, which rarely leads to interesting thoughts. And I have a trust issue with men and women in costume. They feel constricted, both physically and intellectually, in a way that is hard to articulate. When I worked with auditing, I also had to wear a suit and tie for some occasions, with the consequence that I started to talk like R2-D2 and use body language like C-3PO. Not good. Author Tom Rath is on my side, and I think that it's smart to also include others point of view about clothes. In Rath's book *Eat, Move, Sleep* he says:

> While I was working on this book, my grandmother passed away. Even though I knew I was expected to wear a tie at the funeral, I decided not to do it. I simply wanted to be sure that all my energy was focused on what mattered that day: to remember my grandma and be with my family; not feeling strained by an insignificant tie.

My wish is to sometime in the future watch a kind of George Costanza/Jerry Seinfeld duo, who in a playful and relaxed but knowledgeable and deep way discuss the complex world of football. Then I would actually think a football studio is something worthwhile. Is it possible to arrange? I think so. And my go-to example is Sky Sports' Monday Night Football with Ed Chamberlain, Gary Neville, and Jamie Carragher. They have found a dynamic that makes us both laugh and think, but even they have room for growth. Hopefully, one day, their ties will be just a memory (and maybe their suits... and maybe even the host, Ed). Then my dream would be fulfilled.

18 Gratitude?

In her book *Improv Wisdom*, writer Patricia Ryan Madison has an exercise, a thought experiment that she advises everyone to do to increase their level of gratitude. So, I thought we'd try it out. Ask yourself these questions: What products/services help me right now? How have these products/services been created? And what products/services can I show gratitude for right now because they made my life easier?

An example could be: Right now, I'm sitting on a sofa. The sofa was built in China, based on drawings made up by a Danish designer employed by a Swedish furniture giant. Then it was shipped to Sweden by a Dutch transportation company through an intermediary in Germany. In Sweden, the sofa finally arrived at IKEA, from which I sent it home through a UK delivery firm. Thus, there are at least a dozen people and companies I should thank for giving me the opportunity to chill on the divan instead of sitting on the ground.

Another example could be: I watch Arsenal. The Arsenal players train every day (except Tomas Rosicky, who is probably injured) in order to deliver the best football possible. FA (the English Football Association) has arranged so that Arsenal can play football against other top teams in England (in the so-called Premier League). A couple of broadcasters have also made it possible for people abroad to watch Arsenal, and sometimes Gary Neville also provides detailed analyses of the games.

The conclusion is quite clear: There are opportunities for us football fans to show more gratitude, really, but to philosophize about the moral correctness of showing gratitude and in fact showing more gratitude are two completely different things. When referee Michael Oliver (who probably in one day works harder than I have in my entire lifetime) makes a bad call against my Arsenal, well, then I freak out. Gratitude for Oliver's attempt to do a good deed for the sport is gone; left is just an angry dude who cannot understand what function Michael Oliver has in this world.

For those of us who are emotionally unstable when it comes to football, it's hard to show gratitude to the sport we love, at least when the match is still going. To make it easier, perhaps this exercise can be done one hour after each match instead of in the heat of the battle? Or a day after the game? Or at least, maybe, once a year? Yes, it will probably be once a year for myself, and then I will probably thank myself because I put up with this shit...

Ps. forget that last sentence above. I was kidding. I love football. In fact. Be grateful for it. Otherwise you wouldn't have received this divine text. And I would have done something else on my sofa...

19 Context.

Let's skip a long and boring intro and a bit like a punk song jump straight into the action with a quote from the brilliant but unfortunately deceased comedian George Carlin:

> I'm a big supporter of context. I think you can joke about anything if it's done in the right way. Rape is a very difficult subject for 3-4 minutes, but if you have created a context - and that includes not only the context that you created for the joke, but also the larger context, your act, your persona that the audience knows when purchasing the ticket - if all this is in place, then you can ... let's say "manage" it. You will still get some

> people to frown, but they will be with you when you make your next joke.

And to make my point, which I will go into more deeply below, even more clearly, we can listen to a quote from Dr. Marty Klein's book *Sexual Intelligence*:

> One thing that allows people to have passionate sex, without having to think about the "usual" rules that apply in a relationship, is that you are sure that you will return to the normal rules when you are finished. Similarly, it is ok to have a competitive tennis match if we know that everything will be normal afterwards. Thus, we lob the ball up high if our opponent has the sun in his eyes, but after the game we don't toss their car keys into the bushes, out of reach.

Why these quotes? Are you worried that I'm on my way to a somewhat strange journey in this text? Relax, I'll explain what I mean. To summarize the two quotes above, in different contexts, different rules apply. This is important to understand. Here's an example: To smile at another person is usually positive. But if you pull out a really big Zlatan Ibrahimovic smile in the midst of an emotional speech at a funeral, then it could be perceived as a little psychopathic.

Thus, context is something that you want both football players and football fans to be aware of. An interesting case is when the then Manchester City striker Emmanuel Adebayor scored against Arsenal, a club he had left a couple of months earlier (the summer of 2009). Instead of celebrating the goal with his home fans, Adebayor ran across the field and slid down on his knees in front of the Arsenal fans. The event was obviously a huge talking point weeks to come, and Adebayor, who already before (and during) the game was quite unpopular, was suddenly, by far, the biggest nemesis for most Arsenals supporters.

Let's start by looking at this from the Arsenal fans' side. Emmanuel Adebayor went during the summer to Manchester City, a team where players with high salary expectations go. In addition, Adebayor had been pretty lousy during his final season at Arsenal, often walking around with lazy, uninspired body language, prompting fans to question the Togolese even before the sale.

And to the event itself: The traditional behavior, which is also the expected behavior, when a player scores a goal against a team that he previously represented is that the player tries to hold back his instinctive joy in order to pay his respects to his previous relationships. Rejoicing with his own club's fans is clearly a big NO. To cheer in front of his former club's fans is an even a bigger NO. To rush at full speed across the field and then slide down on his knees in front of his former club's fans is thus an action that is clearly beyond normal; an insult; a provocation. Considering this, it is easy to understand why Arsenal fans felt a pretty strong animosity for a few minutes towards Adebayor.

Now, let's instead look at all this based on Adebayor's point of view, and we do this by listening to the protagonist himself, who in an interview had to explain what his emotional life looked like before and during the match:

> It was a special game because I played against my old teammates, who I saw as my brothers. When I got to the playing tunnel and saw my friends, I tried to shake

hands with them... but they didn't want to, which was a shock to me. I wondered: What is happening? What have I done? You know what I mean? I felt hurt. After that, I thought – OK, that's life and you just have to accept it. But when I came onto the field, and heard the Arsenal fans sing condescending songs about my dad and mom, I felt unable to cope with it all. We are after all human beings, and there are some things that are hard to accept. We have our limits. You can insult me, you can judge me as a footballer, this is normal. But leave my parents out of it – I love them more than anything on earth. So when I heard these songs that insulted my family, I thought that I must answer them in some way: But in what way? I can't go in among the fans and start screaming, so a better way is to score goals. And that's what I did. Then my feelings took over, and my celebration was what it was.

Both the fans' and Adebayor's reactions during the game are somehow reasonable. Not divine, but reasonable, because a football stadium is like an emotion machine, where logic rarely makes itself heard. What is interesting is how the two parties reacted after the game. In the Arsenal fans' eyes, Adebayor was some kind of Sauron, but the main character himself was remorseful: "I regret how I celebrated; it was a big mistake."

So, while one party understood that emotions took over and he reacted in a way he shouldn't, the other party, the fans, had a hard time seeing their part in the game. For these people, the game wasn't over; for these people, there was still hatred that made it impossible to self-reflect.

My idea about this is that when we look at or play football, we sign an invisible contract. For 90 minutes – and perhaps some extra ones added by the referee – it is ok for us to be a little derailed. We are allowed to feel extreme joy, but this also means that we can feel stronger feelings of hate than we normally do. But if we go along with this invisible contract, it is important that we understand that it only applies during the match. If we stay in a hateful mood afterwards, it immediately becomes more problematic: We start to flirt with the dark side of our personality, the one that is angry and rarely forgives other people.

And this, of course, applies both to the players and the fans, even though it's more often the fans who don't really understand that the football game is over and that it now is time to behave a little more controlled again. That means don't yell, "You are a cunt!" or write in some football forum that our team "is a bunch of whores." New context!

Let us never forget the fantastic in being a little psychopathic over those one and a half hours, but let us also never forget that we are doing it in a particular context. It's when we begin to blur these boundaries that people begin to question the whole football culture. And that's when it becomes a little bit more difficult to defend the sport that I love endlessly.

20 Finding flow.

It is not that I am ashamed of it, but my cousin Kalle mentioned to me a while ago that I, around 2008, clearly declared that Arsenal's midfield terrier, Mathieu Flamini, was a man for my dream team. Now, of course, you can have your objections to this nomination; it may feel a bit too simplistic, especially considering that I am an Arsenal fan. But fast-forward the tape to 2009, and now Manchester United's Darren Fletcher was on my dream team. You see, there's a connection here, and I'll try to sort it out below.

The Hungarian professor Mihaly Csikzentmihalyi (pronounced Mee-high-ee Chick-sent-me-high-ee) has written a bunch of books on the phenomenon of "flow": a term which basically describes the feeling we have when we do something without thinking of anything else; a stage when we are, according to Csikzentmihalyi, the happiest. In the book *Finding Flow*, he writes:

> Contrary to what we usually think, the best moments in life are not passive, even though such moments could be lovely if we have worked hard to achieve them. The best moments, when we achieve a flow, occur rather when our body and brain have tested their limits in a voluntary effort to achieve something challenging and rewarding.

My (brilliant) thought is that hard-working players like Flamini and Fletcher are more frequently in a flowing stage than other types of players as they have a tendency to give more of themselves on the pitch. They tackle, run, shout – they are constantly active, no matter whether they have the ball or not. And because they are often in a flow state, they're more likely to spread this feeling to their fellow players as a kind of positive virus, and suddenly their whole team is put into a flow state. Their extreme hunger affects and influences a football game in an almost metaphysical way.

Someone who challenged himself and others more than perhaps anyone else was Flamini and Fletcher's big idol – Roy Keane. "As soon as you enter the field, there is only one thing in your head," he said once. "Winning. It's all about hunger. If a player that earns 50 pounds a week has more hunger than me, I'm in danger." Keane is, at least in my view, the godfather of flow. And the interesting thing about that thought is that it probably goes against the general perception of Roy Keane. The vast majority of people that saw Keane probably thought, "Wow, he looks angry. Very angry. He can't feel good," which I believe is a false way of thinking. Instead, I believe Roy Keane, and players like him, are more often the ones who feel best during matches because they have invested the most mental and physical energy. They have no other thoughts beyond the activity itself. Therefore, it is also wrong to believe that we must give the hard workers extra attention for their style of play because they are already satisfied; they had more flow than any of the other players.

And perhaps it was this flow-thought that made me include Flamini on my Dream Team that day in 2008. Maybe I felt that the other stars on my fictional team needed help with flow; that with Flamini on their team they also would get to experience the beauty of being plunged into a perfect headspace. So Kalle, now you have my explanation.

21 A brief theory of Lionel Messi's greatness.

[The end of a text published in GOAL number 7/2012]

...my theory, which really isn't that original, but which I think could be a great help in understanding Messi's greatness, is explained below.

We can begin by listening to a quote from the protagonist himself:

> My style has always been the same. I never tried to develop a particular style of play. From a very young age, I played in the way that came naturally. And even though I learned a lot of tactical ideas when I came to Barcelona I was allowed to always play with great freedom.

You don't even have to read between the lines to come to the conclusion: Messi never really had to change who he is. This conclusion is important to understand. He had the chance to develop his skills entirely organically, and therefore has been able to play with the rhythm that he felt comfortable with. This is relatively uncommon, as players from an early age often are limited by different systems and various tactical plans that stifle the natural creativity in their body. Fortunately for Messi, he was always way better than his teammates, and as a consequence all his coaches never saw any other resort then to give him full liberty; the same freedom Aleksander Hleb had in his first spell in Stuttgart, Ricardo Quaresma in Porto, Matthew Le Tissier in

Southampton, Yossi Benayoun in West Ham, and Juan Roman Riquelme in Villareal. There are hundreds of examples, but the point can be made anyway: Creative players are at their best in an environment where they can follow their own rhythm, and where they have the full confidence of teammates and coaches to express themselves.

Often creative players are at their best on slightly smaller clubs. However, there are a few players on this earth who are so brilliant that they have that same freedom on quality teams. Zlatan Ibrahimovic and Cristiano Ronaldo are two such cases. Messi is a third. Together, the three of them are also three of the world's best players. So, one could easily come to the conclusion that: great team + freedom = world-class player.

My thoughts are slightly anarchistic, and I really want to call attention to the fact that freedom from authority makes it possible for people to achieve their ultimate potential. This idea is to some degree influenced by the Swiss philosopher Rousseau's ideas about human nature, which I recently read, but just as much from my own experiences. My days have better flow – and become more exciting – if I'm allowed to express myself freely, but this is of course difficult in a society that wants people who are molded into a standardized form, after a certain norm. As Rousseau put it: "Freedom is the power to choose our own chains."

This is my conclusion to this text, and I hope you had a nice time. What I hope you have gleaned from this portrait is that: a) Messi is a fantastic role model for all young (and old) people; and b) Besides being a nice guy with good values, he is also living proof of what can happen if you let your natural characteristics grow at their own pace and on their own terms.

Then you can create inexplicably beautiful things.

22 Oscar 2.0.

When I write, I often imagine a smarter version of myself sitting in an armchair opposite me. My thought is simply: What would Oscar 2.0 think of this? What kind of texts would get him to look at me in admiration and shout, "This is gold, Oscar, this is pure gold!"?

The idea is to liberate myself from what other people consider to be a good text. There are more than seven billion people on this earth, and therefore as many ways of seeing the world, which means that my thoughts more often than not will be out of sync with a couple of billion people. If I were to go for a 100-percent "hit rate," a must-be-adored-by-all-attitude, I would probably have mental problems.

For example: How many different articles (not to mention forum posts) do you think are posted after a match between, let's say, Manchester City and Manchester United? I don't have the exact answer, but the more vague answer is "many." Or "numerous." Hundreds of thousands of people express their views, and somewhere in all that mud we sometimes forget that most of those hundreds of thousands of opinions are pretty unqualified – "noise" is the term that Gary Neville would use. But the interesting thing is that many footballers seem to read what is written in the newspapers and on the web, and they are affected by the prevailing views among supporters and bad journalists (that usually love to criticize, as negative criticism is so much easier to give than praise).

I mean, I hope that the players have a sense where valuable analysis should come from. Not from the media, come on! It ought to be from other players or their coach, who live in the same world and have roughly the same sense of what an accomplishment in that world means, and thus (at least in 99% of cases) have a more informed assessment basis than journalists and supporters. As the standup giant Brian Regan says, "when other comedians like what you do, it's the ultimate compliment." But again, I would like to take that quote and add that whenever YOU like what you do, that is the ultimate compliment.

The question then becomes: What is needed to be able to make a reasonable assessment of yourself? The answer: an ounce of self-reflection and self-awareness. I truly believe that many players can manage themselves quite well without receiving any evaluation from their coach. If we look at the tennis world and Roger Federer, it's interesting to see how he, during different periods, has played brilliant tennis without a coach. Why can he do that? Extreme self-knowledge (he must have read Ralph Waldo Emerson's *Self-Reliance* because he definitely lives by Emerson's doctrine). No one needs to tell Federer why his forehand is somewhat mistimed on a particular day. He knows. And even if he doesn't know exactly, he probably knows better than anyone else. With extreme self-knowledge à la Federer there also comes freedom. Suddenly, you don't care that much about what others say and think; instead, there is a reflection about the self that is much more complex than other people's (often) superficial assessments, which means that whenever you like something you do, it is the ultimate compliment.

Personally, as I said in the beginning, I use Oscar 2.0. He is pretty sharp, not as sloppy and lazy as me. When he doesn't like something, I know it's crap; when he likes something, it is usually ok.

So what does he think about this text? To be honest, he isn't completely satisfied, but he hasn't "deleted" the text either, which means that I will allow it to be part of this essay collection.

23 In a park far away from Old Trafford.

What is "real" football?

This is a question that on paper looks a little bit silly, but I think you understand what I mean when I ask it. But let's reformulate it: When and where can you find the most authentic football?

I'm sitting outside an old pub in the village of Aldea on the southwest coast of Gran Canaria (obviously with a beer, cigarette, and in a romantic mood – a tragic attempt to be as much Henry Miller as I can), and after a while my eyes move to an open area in a park where a bunch of kids are kicking a football. The field that they built consists of four shirts that clearly signal whether there are throw-ins or corners, and two shoes and two water bottles that mark where they can score.

The rules are, however, somewhat unclear. One of the boys gets pulled down, and suddenly they form a playful rugby pile. The plan's smallest player, a 6-7-year-old kid with way too much hair (think Vince Neil in Mötley Crüe), refuses to participate in the pile, instead running with the ball towards the opponent's goal and scoring while the others are still fully occupied with getting higher and higher up the rugby pile. Fifteen minutes later, one of the boys' dads drop by and he screams, "Juan, la hora de cena!" Juan, the most outgoing guy in the group, with a voice as intense as Jamie Carragher, makes a sad face to his buddies. Time to go home, eat dinner, and be bored.

One of the most outspoken people in today's stand-up scene is American comedian Doug Stanhope. He is a man who has an opinion on everything, which means that he also has a view on so-called "real" laughter:

> I get onstage, and it just all seems like a fucking scam. What "funny" really is to me is hanging out with other comics around a table. Real, genuine "comedy" is making the guy stocking shelves at Walmart laugh when he's having a shitty day. You just say shit no one else ever says and you break the social mold and make someone laugh or guffaw or gasp on the job when they don't expect it. Then it means something. The only time it's truly rewarding is when you make someone laugh just cause you wanted to, then you leave. You don't ask them to buy a CD in return, you know? That's how it is when comedians are just hanging out: no commerce, no

"job to do," just some funny shit we're giving away free to each other and laughing our asses off.

Without sounding like a communist, which is always a risk when one contradicts capitalism, there is something problematic with the ridiculous sums of money spinning around in today's football. This isn't an original thought: I think everybody knows about it; if not in the brain, in the heart. Money does something with the creative vein – like a cancer, it has a tendency to slowly destroy our innate magic. When Manchester United and Chelsea face each other on a Sunday afternoon it's kind of like when Doug Stanhope goes up on a stage somewhere in the United States. Through a well thought out formula, they deliver quality on time – the audience has paid for that. But is that the ultimate football experience?

Actually we know. We know when we are doing something meaningful. We know when we feel real emotions. When we do something we love just because we love it – not because we need to. Cristiano Ronaldo knows this. Lionel Messi knows this. But it is of course difficult for them to really enjoy football the way they did when they were young and free from their current job description. Football culture, as it looks today, almost forces the players to think with a market economy mindset – a mindset that in practice makes it impossible for them to feel the authenticity of, say, a day in the park.

Sometimes, however, I get the feeling that there's a little authenticity out there among all the bureaucracy, especially in Germany. Clubs such as Borussia Dortmund, St. Pauli, and Freiburg try their best to bring qualitative values instead of quantitative values into their organizations. Coaches like Jürgen Klopp and Christian Streich are therefore spiritual leaders for those of us who hope for a paradigm shift; for those of us who yearn for something more deep, stripped of all the crap that comes when socially constructed concepts like "money" become too large a part of the players' and coaches' mindset, which diminishes their original love of football.

We'll see what happens, for who knows what football will look like in 10-20 years? One guess is that it will not have changed that much. Que sera, sera. But I hope to see a slow introduction of softer values in football institutions; values that bring us closer to the playful (but still competitive) football that Juan and his buddies are playing in a park somewhere in Aldea. A football that is based on fun and freedom, and sometimes, when you least expect it, rugby piles.

24 Hypothetically.

A random man has spoken with you for two hours down at the pub. One beer has become a few beers. You have discussed life. Love. And you've obviously been discussing football. He begins to find out your views on things: your life philosophy, your football philosophy. You're now beginning to talk about your favorite players. You will first drop two names that will make him feel, "aha, I think I would have been able to guess that by what you've been saying during our conversation," and then, from out of the blue, you will drop two names that will cause him to think, "oh, shit, you're a more complex person than I thought." What are your first choices? And which players are a little more shocking that you appreciate? Will you reveal your secret love for Joe Allen? Or Nacho Monreal? And what do your choices say about you as a person?

25 The Man in the Glass.

We all handle stress in different ways, and all ways are, at least for me, interesting. Some meditate or go to intense spinning classes; others order a dozen beers at some cozy pub and then make love to a fat stranger. I judge no one. The manager of Sheffield United, Nigel Adkins, has perhaps picked the most poetic option of all. When Nigel (then in Southampton) before a match against Tottenham in 2012 was asked by a reporter how he handles stress, he replied quickly:

When you get what you want in your struggle for self
And the world makes you king for a day
Just go to the mirror and look at yourself
And see what that man has to say.

For it isn't your father, or mother, or wife
Whose judgment upon you must pass
The fellow whose verdict counts most in your life
Is the one staring back from the glass.

He's the fellow to please – never mind all the rest
For he's with you, clear to the end
And you've passed your most difficult, dangerous test
If the man in the glass is your friend.

You may fool the whole world down the pathway of years
And get pats on the back as you pass
But your final reward will be heartache and tears
If you've cheated the man in the glass.

First, we'll have to make it clear that this isn't a poem created by Nigel; it's the American composer Dale Wimbrow who put these beautiful words together, which have touched millions of people. Second, Nigel's performance when he read it wasn't that good: there was rather a David Brent vibe (for those of you who haven't seen the *Office*, do it now, because you should, and then you will understand the reference) as he recited Wimbrow's poem. And third, Adkins was fired two months later.

But all this is perhaps unimportant? For it is Nigel Adkins' stoic way of managing stress that appeals to me. He knows that he lives by his values, which makes him more "anti-fragile," a phrase that I steal from author Nassim Nicholas Taleb, i.e., someone who can thrive in a complex world where chance is a key factor. The use of the poem "The Man in the Glass" as a tool for being more anti-fragile is perfect. So, I'm thinking strongly of snatching this method: Taping up this poem on my fridge, reading it aloud and slowly, and then living a life according to my own manufactured values.

Not one where I cheated "The Man in the Glass."

26 A quasi-spiritual thought about tactics.

When I read an interview with the brilliant comedian Bill Burr on the website Splitinsider.com, I liked his way of describing how his act was formed: "Your act is almost like you're playing tag. Your act is the base, where you're safe. So, you just kind of run around, improv it, and if all of a sudden, if it's starting to go bad, you just go back to your act."

The essence of the quote is basically: Improvise, but have a foundation to fall back on. It is important in comedy, and perhaps even more important in football.

I think you can see when a team has a deep understanding of the game, and for each other: like Arsenal around 2003; as Barcelona five years later; as Bayern Munich anno 2013. These teams were so called "self-playing pianos." Sure, they all had skillful coaches, but also you (unless "you" are my brother) and I would have been able to do pretty well with these teams: it wouldn't, in any case, have been all that impressive if we had done well, because they were teams that didn't need to be reminded of basic football knowledge; teams that stood above base ABC tactics, and thus could create something much more interesting, something magical, at least now and then, which couldn't be described in theory.

The game of football is fluid. It's in the sport's DNA that when you get to a certain level, too many tactics only hinder you from stretching your limits; the label "right back" will stifle your movement patterns, and more instructions will limit the choices that you can make on the field. So, the more advanced a player is, the more he need the right mindset, instead of a dozen tactical directives, something that Arsenal's coach, Arsene Wenger, knows well; Wenger, who never gives particularly rich instructions to his players before the match. The results might go against him sometimes, but his philosophy can also create a group like "The Invincibles," which was one of last decade's most beautiful teams. Where players flowed freely between lines; where the coach relied on the players' individual abilities to make the right decisions in the moment (which of course doesn't work unless you have an extremely tight group with an already deep tactical knowledge base).

Tactics will always be interesting for us beginners. I'm a beginner at too many things, which means that I sometimes need guidance – "to-do" lists – even though I hate them. And rich instructions will always be interesting to teams that lack a clear philosophy, à la Barcelona; teams who struggles to understand the game;

who need a framework, an act to come back to. In the end, hopefully, after having dedicated their souls completely to the football God and achieving deep tactical knowledge, maybe they can reach the Barca magic, the magic that can only happen when we go past basic tactics and move into a more structure-free Nietzsche universe. But only then.

Wishy-washy? Absolutely, but what did you expect from a quasi-spiritual Arsene Wenger fan? Maybe I should, however, have used a better tactic with this text; perhaps it was simply too much play... and maybe I forgot to get back to my act in time....

27 Lonely, I'm so lonely.

[Posted on Fotbollskanalen.se March 8, 2011]

Celebrated goalkeeper, popular among teammates, loved by wife and children. To be honest, life is not that awful if your name is Victor Valdes.

From being a good goalkeeper, Victor Valdes has now become a goalie that some – but not me – even consider better than Iker Casillas. He is the last brigade of a team that could go down in history as one of the finest teams to have ever walked on this planet. But the fairytale of Victor Valdes was about to end abruptly way, way earlier... so let us start from the beginning.

It all started one day in the late 80s, when his brother, Ricardo Valdes, was in great need of a goalkeeper: To shoot without a goalie is, in all honesty, pretty fucking boring in the long run. Ricardo knew that his younger brother did everything he said, and Victor did of course take the chance to socialize with his older, slightly cooler, brother and agreed to guard the garage door. Once became twice, and suddenly it became a routine that Ricardo placed his little brother in the goal.

Victor's father, Jose Manuel Valdes, sometimes went out to have a look at what his sons were doing, and he started to see that his youngest son was very brave: Victor refused to give away easy goals and threw himself, totally fearless, at everything that came his way.

Signs that Victor could be a very capable goalie had appeared.

After a stop in a smaller local club, Victor arrived at FC Barcelona, where his skills impressed the youth coach Salvadore Riera. The problem was that at home Victor complained; he didn't understand why he had to be in goal. When the team scored, he didn't feel involved. When the opponents scored, there was a risk that he would be reviled. What was in it for Victor? Father Valdes called Salvadore and reported Victor's thoughts about quitting and asked if the coach could try to persuade his son. Children are usually pretty easy to brainwash, and after a pep talk, Salvadore convinced Valdes to continue. But the doubt was still there.

When Victor Valdes left for La Masia as a 10 year old, he was devastated. His family decided to move to Tenerife, and Victor, who was only a child, had to make a decision to stay in Barcelona, Catalonia, or join the family. He did stay, largely thanks to his father, who from an early age had planted the dream of becoming a soccer star in Victor's brain. But he loved his family; he hated being away from them. And pretty soon he realized that La Masia was not the paradise that he painted in his young, somewhat naive, mind: "Sometimes I didn't understand why I needed to be away from my family, because I felt so good when I was with them."

Five months passed, five months of phone calls, especially in the evenings, which were both long and relatively tough for everyone involved. A couple of times the family visited Victor, but it didn't help that much – the young goalkeeper was homesick.

After barely six months at La Masia, Victor's quality of life had hit rock bottom, and a one-way ticket back to his family in Tenerife was Victor's solution. At home, he started to rebel against his father and the football world. He was tired of football, and his father had to fight to get him to training sessions. But one day in the magical summer of 1994, Victor was sitting with his family in front of the TV and tuned in to Canal Plus. His old teammates in Barcelona were playing a youth tournament, and the commentators were quite lyrical as they discussed Barca's rampage. Instead of feeling the delight of his teammates, Victor shut the TV off and went to his room and started to cry: "I was after all a part of the team and I regretted very much that I wasn't there, to be a part of what I saw was a privilege in that moment – to be on TV and all that."

The grass is always greener on the other side, at least according to young Victor Valdes. Now he was determined to get back to Barcelona. He trained twice a day: in the morning with the local team, in the afternoon with his father on the beach. The training was intense, but the hard workouts with his father made him strong, and at age 13 it was time to return to the club that made him hate football: Barcelona.

At first it worked fine. He was happy to see all his friends and to get a second chance in life, which many people don't get. But the games started to become less fun, winning began to mean everything, and his feelings of anxiety grew stronger: "It was a state of anxiety created by thinking about the weekend's match. It made me next to nauseous to think that it was a game this Saturday. And I knew that the 90 minutes would be terrible." And it didn't help that his teammates were relaxed and joked before the game. Victor felt isolated in his anxiety:

> You saw teammates in a happy state, laughing, because they would be playing a game of football. I was the child who didn't enjoy it that much. You end up thinking that this life maybe isn't for me. That maybe there are other paths in life. And sometimes I dreamed only about being just a regular player, not a keeper – to be like all of my friends.

It wasn't until he was 18 years old that he told other people about his dark thoughts about football. Therapy plus the tremendous support of his family managed to take Victor past the stage where he wanted to quit football.

Today, with five league titles, a couple of Champions League trophies, and various other knick-knacks, he can probably say that he is living in a dream.

But one thing is certain: It was never his childhood dream.

Ps. By the way, if you've got a minute or two. A man named Joaquin got the idea a few years ago to create a song with lyrics that highlight how amazing Victor Valdes is in every way. The name of the song is Victor Valdes (El Numero Uno) and is actually quite catchy. Unfortunately, my Spanish is at a level where, at best, I can order a watery Spanish beer at a small bar, so I don't get all the lyrics, but I get the feeling that there are many positively charged words included in this serenade. Listen and enjoy.

28 My ultimate dream.

I am at a masquerade (something I hate...), and I have an energy level that is scary low. There is nothing, absolutely nothing that could make me feel good. Why am I here? Just when my misery reaches a new low, which I thought couldn't possibly happen, I see a man dressed as Francesco Totti on the other side of the room. My natural football-geek instinct takes over and makes me walk up to him. He says this, I say that, and suddenly I am in the midst of a conversation I never want to end. I think, "Who are you? The world's best?"

and walk away from the magic conversation with a Santi Cazorla smile.

Why is it like this? I mean, I'm a pretty normal guy: I like music, movies, traveling, psychology, philosophy, and many other things. I'm not entirely abnormal (even though others argue that this is up for debate). But something happens to me when I stumble into a real football geek: It's like I don't even need to push myself; no energy needs to be sacrificed; everything has a nice flow. And in cases where my energy is low, a good football conversation can fill up my energy tank in just a few minutes. It's crazy.

In a perfect world, or at least a perfect world for me, everyone would be a football expert. Imagine how easy my life would be. No need to search for an obscure topic that both people are interested in when you start a conversation. No shallow dialogues about the weather, where both parties have that "I am slowly dying here" feeling. Instead, just a big fat cocktail of glowing energy that arises when two people have the freedom to talk about what they love the most. And in this case, that would always be football.

Maybe it's just a utopian dream? And maybe it isn't even desirable? Maybe we want to have conversations about everything, just like the renaissance ideal? Ok, fair point. My point, however, is that we could connect all other subjects to football. We could discuss anxiety, and then use Arsene Wenger as an example; or depression and Sebastian Diesler; or why not creativity and Luis Suarez (alternatively, otology and Luis Suarez).

In the same way that different countries probably would feel more connected if they spoke the same language, I think it would be interesting to see what happened if everyone, in addition to his or her regular hobbies, was also a football geek. Don't you think it would be a more beautiful world, with more connections between people? Something we all long for.

I think we should start the revolution now. At the next party you're at, refuse to talk about anything other than football. Every time someone tries to discuss something else, cut him or her off and start to explain why there is good evidence that Dennis Bergkamp is the son of God. Maybe you won't do it. That's ok. But in my dreams we all speak about football. And dress in Totti shirts.

29 Religious enthusiasm.

There are many ways to show Barcelona's quality. One can endlessly discuss their beautiful technique, their movement, or how amazing they are at producing world-class players from their famous youth academy (even though it has been a while). An angle that is interesting, however, is the one that the Liverpool coach Jürgen Klopp has been looking at – Barcelona's way of acting after scoring: "One thing I do quite often is to show my players pictures of Barcelona when they celebrate a goal. Why is that? You see them celebrate goal 5868 as if it were the first goal they ever scored. This is what you should always feel – until you die."

When Leo Messi scores a goal, it shouldn't, at least in theory, be that surprising or special. All the statistics show that it is pretty likely that Messi will score. But still, when he scores, Gerard Pique runs at 120 km/h to celebrate with him, Andres Iniesta's eyes get anime big, and the protagonist himself looks like a teenage girl meeting Harry from One Direction for the first time. There's almost a Spring Break vibe.

The famous British writer Aldous Huxley, who wrote the dystopian novel *Brave New World*, once said "the secret of genius is to carry the spirit of a child into old age, which means never losing your enthusiasm." If Barcelona is a good example of this youthful enthusiasm in football, the next example is perhaps even more fitting. I speak of course about Filippo "Pippo" Inzaghi: The man who never stopped celebrating. Without going through the whole bio of Inzaghi, even though we could spend days digging deep into his strange character, we can mention that the Italian legend (don't question the word "legend," please) for two decades put fear into all defenders every time he entered the penalty are (an area he seldom left). And he scored. Often. He was Super Pippo: hated by many, loved by more.

With Inzaghi, it becomes a little bit more complex than with the Barca case. To celebrate something, to show that you care about the activity you are participating in, is usually something that is appreciated, because people who don't care about anything at all are borderline psychopaths. But if you care too much, your emotions will direct how you behave, which means that you're only a small step from being rather childish. This is why Inzaghi is an interesting case: constantly on the border between charming and obnoxious; hated and loved at the same time (there are few players, if any, that are so often mentioned with the words "love/hate" in the same sentence as Inzaghi). It did not matter if it was the decisive goal in a Champions League semifinal or a 5-0 goal in a meaningless Serie A match – his celebration looked the same. Pure ecstasy.

After a little too crazy celebration against Torino many years ago, Inzaghi actually felt sorry; he understood that he had acted a bit disrespectful to the opponents. But he had an explanation: "For me, every goal I score is a religious experience – I can't consciously control what happens after I score."

Unreasonable? Hmmm. There may be a point here that could be worth holding onto for a while. People who fall into ecstasy are often overcome with a feeling that the world is dramatically altered, that laws and rules are redundant, and now they are in tune with a higher and more important force, which means that their rational "I" is, for a while, disconnected. Through the centuries, philosophers have been concerned about so-called irrational people like Inzaghi, those who aren't really able to control all their emotions with their rational brain. A "perfect" person, according to Western philosophers, is lightly melancholic and rarely reaches any form of ecstasy. It's dangerous.

But some could not resist playing with the idea of the ecstatic man. Like Friedrich Nietzsche. His idea of Dionysus and Apollo, two ancient gods with multifarious natures, where Dionysus (think Antonio Cassano) stands for passion and drunkenness while Apollo (think Louis van Gaal) stands for order and structure, caused artists to see creation in a new way. Nietzsche thought that the best pieces of art were created in the harmony between the wild and the structured: just as with Barcelona, where enthusiastic players operate from a stable structure; where ecstasy and order form some kind of synthesis, something higher, something better. I love that mixture. And I am fully aware that there has to be some sort of structure, tactics, and order in football. But in a world full of indifference, I thirst for passion; I thirst for people (or animals) whose eyes glow; Inzaghis, who send our world into flux, which makes the earth a more dynamic place to live; those that make me feel. Sometimes these people might disgust us a little bit, but who cares? That may be necessary if we want to experience something magical.

For as the brilliant, and always quotable, philosopher/writer Ralph Waldo Emerson wrote: "Nothing great was ever created without enthusiasm." And no Inzaghis will be created without religious enthusiasm.

30 Much Adu about nothing.

[Published in the GOAL number 5/2013]

To become a superstar in football, you usually need a mix of the right DNA and the right environment. If you don't have a natural ability to move around on the field, it will be difficult to reach the very top, but that doesn't mean that those who have an extreme natural ability automatically get there either.

I considered myself to be talented, but too lazy. A bit like Matthew Le Tissier (even tried to get my teammates to call me "Le God"...). I'm one of those who sit around the campfire and brag about "how bad luck stopped me from being a superstar." Very charming... But the coming stories aren't about me; they are about three of the biggest talents from the last decade, who didn't quite reach the heights we all believed they were destined for.

At the beginning of the new millennium, there was a name that was perhaps a little hotter than everyone else's – Sebastian Deisler. Germany had, after an unsuccessful 1998 World Cup and an even worse Euro 2000, looked for a man they could advertise to the people as "the new Beckenbauer." Deisler was perfect in every way.

Let us first define how Deisler was as a footballer. Think of a faster version of David Beckham, who dribbles like Joaquin and reads the game like Philip Lahm. A decent combo, right? So in the early 2000s, the German population thought, "Super, now we finally have a potential world-class player whose talent is somewhat close to Beckenbauer – let's put our hope in him and let him know."

For an injury prone (think Jonathan Woodgate) and introverted (think Lionel Messi) teenage Deisler, the crazy expectations were a nightmare:

> I was 19, 20 years old when the Germans thought that I could save their football. I alone. Today there are five or six players that the German people and the media divide their attention and their hopes on. In those days? Then there was only Michael Ballack, but he was four years older than me and played in the idyllic Kaiserslautern. I was never left alone.

When he went to Bayern Munich in 2002, the pressure became even more intense. Now he was expected to not only lead the national team, but also one of the world's most powerful football empires. It was too much.

In late 2003, Deisler was really down, depressed, and he had to go to a clinic to work out his feelings. Since then, he has never been quite the same person again. The spirit that once existed in Deisler's eyes is gone. In 2007, Deisler announced that he was retiring from football because his love for the world of competitive football had completely disappeared:

> The kind of football that I miss is different from the one I left. I have come to realize that I was not made for this business. In the end I was empty, old, and tired. I ran as far as my legs could carry me. I couldn't do more.

Sebastian Deisler is the perfect example of the dark side of modern football. Let's face it: It's a strange environment that a professional football player usually lives in – with demands from coaches, management, fans, media, and others – and it's a tricky task to create balance and harmony. So, if you are a sensitive person like Deisler, problems will arise. Nowadays, many clubs employ their own psychologist/therapist, but at that time most players didn't have a person in the club that could work with their psyche. A pity, because who knows how many trophies Deisler would have today if he had developed a strong mind to match his talent...

But let's move on, because life is about movement. Around the same time as Deisler joined Bayern Munich, in 2002, two super talents had emerged in Portugal, both playing for the same club, Sporting Lisbon. One was Cristiano Ronaldo. The other, who was considered the biggest talent of the two, was Ricardo Quaresma. Both wingers; both with ridiculously good technique. After a less successful season for Sporting in 2002/2003, Europe's big clubs saw the chance to recruit these two future superstars, and two of the real giants won the battle. Ronaldo went to Manchester United and Quaresma to Barcelona. After that, their journeys differed – yes, one could even say that their careers went in opposite directions.

Ronaldo evolved into a monster, an unstoppable force that would have been called the world's best footballer if it weren't for a short guy from Argentina. Quaresma? Well, he currently plays in Al Ahli Dubai [written before he went to Porto]. And nothing bad about Al Ahli, which is one of the premier teams in the UAE Arabian Gulf League, but there's a difference between Al Ahli and the club he was at a decade ago.

So, what happened? The first thing we can say about Ricardo Quaresma is that he is quite, let's say, hmmmm... opinionated. When there is too much focus on defense and being in the right position, Quaresma doesn't react positively. He wants freedom. If football was an individual sport, Quaresma would have been world class (see a couple of Quaresma YouTube clips and you'll know what I mean). But football is about more than individual skill, which Quaresma has bitterly experienced during his career.

He only played one season at Barcelona, and the big reason why was that he and coach Frank Rijkard had completely different football philosophies. Rijkard, who during his playing career was a defensive midfielder, was not impressed by Quaresma's lack of work on defense. Quaresma, who wanted freedom, felt restricted. After the short spell in Barcelona, Quaresma moved back to Portugal, but this time to Porto. In Porto he excelled, largely due to the confidence that the team manager showed him and the increased freedom he was given, and for four years he was one of the Portuguese league's best players. In 2008, Jose Mourinho became coach of Inter Milan. Mourinho had followed Quaresma's development in Porto and thought the tricky winger was now ready to once again join one of Europe's biggest teams. Inter bought Quaresma for 15 million euros, but six months later the majority of fans wondered why. Quaresma was voted Serie A's second worst player in 2008, and Mourinho wasn't entirely happy with his attitude during the first half of the season: "He's a great talent, but the joy I have in seeing Ibra [Zlatan Ibrahimovic] work for and with the team, I have not experienced yet with Quaresma. He must learn, otherwise he will not play."

After being lent out to Chelsea during the spring of 2009, he had yet another disappointing season at Inter before joining Besiktas in 2010. Here he found the joy of football again: "Of all the clubs I been to, Besiktas is the club I have been the happiest at and felt most at home, no doubt about it."

Everything perfect? Nah, of course not. This is Quaresma we are talking about. After being substituted at halftime in a Europe League match against Ahtletico Madrid, he was angry at coach Carlos Carvalhal. Really pissed. So pissed that he screamed: "I brought you here, you are only thinking about yourself! Unless I was here, you wouldn't be here! You cannot replace me, you're nothing!"

Besiktas had enough of Quaresma's ego in December last year and released him. So, here we are. In Al Ahli. Maybe it was we who misunderstood Quaresma? Perhaps his football life never was about winning the biggest titles? Maybe it was just a show – "The Quaresma Show" – and perhaps it was Dubai that was the logical end goal for this show? But many ask themselves what could have happened, and should have happened, if he had been able to tone down his anarchistic philosophy.

On another continent, a talent arose in the mid-2000s that perhaps was more hyped than any other player ever been. They called him "the Tiger Woods of football," "the man version of Mia Hamm," and "the new Pele." Freddy Adu clearly had a very tumultuous start to his football life. Before he made his first professional match he was signed by Nike, which meant that he was already a millionaire after just 14 years on this planet:

> My mother worked two or three jobs to take care of my brother and me. So if Nike comes to you and says they want to give a million-dollar contract and the MLS wants to make you the highest-paid player at 14, you can't say "no."

The expectations from Nike were ridiculous. Nike founder Phil Knight said in an interview that he expected that Adu would have a greater impact on Nike than basketball giant LeBron James. Natural expectations for a 14 year old. Besides, he wasn't exactly popular among his DC United teammates, where he joined at age 15, because they knew about his salary:

> A lot of the guys in the locker room resented me. It was right in your face. They felt like they'd been around, put their time in, and here comes this 14 year old who's the highest-paid player and the face of the league. They would yell at me for the dumbest reasons.

Nearly 10 years later, Adu is still just a talent. After a few years in the United States, and four relatively unsuccessful years in Europe, he moved back to the US to play for Philadelphia in 2011. Despite more playing time this time around, many felt that Adu still had a hard time finding the right mix between when he would dribble, pass, and shoot. Expert commentator and former national team star Alexis Lalas said: "He [Adu] is kind of like a luxury car. He is just not practical."

Just when I write this, Freddy Adu is headed to Bahia, a club located in Salvador, who plays in the Brazilian top league [and at the time I write THIS, he is in Finland playing for KuPS]. It isn't shocking. Adu is only 23 years, and it would be premature to judge him yet, but the breakthrough that not only Nike but the rest of the football world have been waiting for has to happen soon. So far, it has only been "Much Adu about nothing"...

31 A revolutionary idea!

I have intensively thought about something the last couple of days: Wouldn't it be interesting to have a warm-up field next to the real football field? My thought, which might not be fully developed, is that you could have a sort of warm-up match beside the real match, and when the assistant manager (who keeps track of the warm-up match) sees someone on his team that has found a nice flow, or is about to find it, he gives a signal to the manager to change the flow player into the real game. There are, of course, free substitutions, which means that replaced players can regain their flow and play a vital role later in the game.

It sounds like an idiotic idea. I agree. But I know how difficult it is to start things – everything from lifting the first kettlebell in the gym to reading the opening pages of a heavy James Joyce book. Therefore, we usually don't want to start various activities because we know that the beginning is often extremely tough, and we know that it is impossible to find flow at that time. This is also why I have so much understanding for teams/players whose engine is somewhat slow and sluggish at the start. They are "night people." Their qualities show up later in the game, but they need an extended period of time in which to find the match rhythm, the rhythm in which their bodies are synced to what is happening in the "now." Evening people hate morning people. They are just too lively, almost as if they are on ecstasy, at a time when the evening people are still light years away from their flow.

And this is what motivated my thought about warm-up fields. They would equalize the playing field. Do you understand? Players who have a sluggish start could work on their timing in the warm-up field, and then be thrown into the real game when they found the "zone." This would mean that it could also be a place for us night people in football, because right now, the climate is different, and I get tired, close to irritated when I see some teams start the match at a tempo that is just ridiculous. Come on, take it easy!

Probably this somewhat stupid, but perhaps even brilliant, thought is grounded in the fact that my Arsenal is famous for our sluggish starts. We rarely start the match perfectly: We have too many players who need time to find some kind of rhythm, which means that we are vulnerable at the beginning of the game since no one on our team has a particularly good rhythm. But as I explained above, I understand them. I'm the same. I only wish that the warm-up plan concept had been around when I was young and struggling to get into games. I was a champion, or at least not completely useless, on the training field, where I had all the time in the world to find flow, but in matches I was pretty invisible 70% of the game because my body wasn't ready to deliver before it was ready.

So, are you convinced? Is it time to introduce a warm-up field? As for the details of what it might look like, well, we can work on that later. Right now, they are insignificant. The important thing is that we begin to create a dialogue around this potentially revolutionary idea!

32 Be here now.

I want to start by telling you that I'm semi-obsessed with being present, and I often think about it (which isn't the best, because if you think about being present too much there is a great risk of missing the moment...). Anyway: I meditate. I try to keep myself busy with so-called flow activities. And I drink (sometimes too much). I am simply interested in what happens at the times we stop thinking, and therefore I'm trying to set up a system and language for myself, a kind of doctrine, which easily puts me in the present.

I got stuck reading an interview with Tomas Rosicky – the man with the eternally youthful hairstyle – and especially the part of the interview that dealt with Rosicky's way of looking at his career. He was asked a question about how much he thinks about the future, to which he replied, "I'm trying to play every game like it's going to be my last." If only read fast, the sentence doesn't say that much. But if you slowly, slowly, almost at a snail's pace read it, and also try to go deeper into what it means to have such a mindset, then I think you will find something interesting; possibly a feeling of relief, possibly a fear of death, possibly something else.

Many thousands of years ago humans obviously lived in a completely different way than today. Improvisation was a greater virtue than foresight – every day was different depending on where you went and what you chased. To plan too much was simply not effective. Somewhere along the way, however, something happened, a paradigm shift – some dude found out that you could store food, and as a consequence it was no longer a necessity to seek new places to hunt all the time. Smart! But this was also the end of the period in which improvisation was our primary way of evolving; where chaos was embraced. Now we have meeting calendars instead. We learned to intelligently plan the day to avoid starvation, but we also learned to worry about the future. In today's society, this is perhaps worse than ever: We have more calendars around us than we can count; we are constantly connected to devices (read: computers/phones) that are efficiently designed to minimize improvising; and to call a friend on Friday and ask him or her to go for a pub crawl that same night and get the answer "Absolutely!" is about as likely as seeing Luis Suarez and Patrice Evra cuddle with lit candles, cheese, and wine.

Maybe I'm exaggerating, but you get the point.

People have meetings. And they plan for the future. And they worry about different outcomes in the future. But I think there is a paradox here, one that Tomas Rosicky seems to be aware of. That is to say, the more we are in the present, the more beneficial it is for our future. And vice versa. Eckhart Tolle, a self-help writer, formulated this paradox perfectly in his book *A New Earth*:

> When you are present, when your attention is fully in the Now, this Presence will transform what you do. There will be quality and power to your actions. You are present when your actions aren't just a means to an end (money, prestige, winning), but is satisfying in itself, when there is joy and vibrancy in what you do.

The next time you see an elite athlete perform at the highest level, it's pretty likely that he or she has abandoned the past and the future and instead focused solely on what is happening in front of his or her eyes. When Tiger Woods holes a chip shot on the 16th hole at Augusta, or when Djokovic hits a forehand on the line in the deciding set against Federer, you know what happens. The power of being in the "Now" is strong.

We don't know if Rosicky practices what he preaches, though I believe it, but at least he gives himself the opportunity to think differently by speaking in such language as "I try to play every game as if it were my last." Like James Bond accentuates every moment; like Henry Miller wrote in the book *Black Spring*, "...act as if even the next step was the last..." That's probably where it all starts.

And let's be serious, being involved in football is actually not a bad idea since the sport itself is one of the greatest tools for being present. Spiritually rewarding you could almost say. Tell that to your so-called "spiritual" friends the next time you see them.

33 Trial and error.

Ok? Are you ready for an adventure? Because each quote from comedian Patrice O'Neal, who sadly passed away in 2011, is an adventure, and this quote from the fantastic book *Satiristas* is one of my favorites:

> My audience trust me; they know I will not disappoint them. Even when I do less good stuff, they think, "Fuck it, try whatever you feel like. We know that you are trying to take us to an exciting place and we want to go there with you ."

For a comedian, it is the ultimate situation to be in: Your audience knows your persona, which means that they have no doubt that you will ultimately find something exciting, something captivating to talk about, even though it might take a while for you to get there. It's called trust. This is something that is equally important in the world of football: A player who knows that he can make mistakes and still retain his starting place will shine; he has a mental freedom that opens up all his hidden potential; he tries and tries until he understands what the ultimate solution is.

Players who are afraid, those who don't have trust from the coach, will over analyze. They will in every situation try to maximize the love from the coach, which ultimately will mean that they minimize the love from the coach, one of the paradoxes of life, as they seek perfection before they have gone through the necessary failure phase: the "trial and error" phase that provides you with the necessary information to achieve something that at least sometimes is close to perfection. As long as players are reasonably intelligent, a mistake is an extremely valuable source of information, as Louis CK (whom I love, but possibly quote too much in my life) knows – and formulates a lot better than me:

> I've always said it, that you learn more from mistakes than from successes. Take my first film Pootie Tang as an example: I got to make a movie finally, which was my dream, and it was terrible, and then it got made even more terrible, and then it came out, and I was just hated. I mean, the first time I was known by a lot of people was because I made a bad movie. But the great thing is that after maybe a week it just goes away, and all

you're left with is the forensic evidence of all the mistakes you made and all of the rocks that you've kind of crashed into, and you're left with this beautiful map of where all the dangers are, and you repair all the holes, and then you're so much better.

So: How do we get as many players as possible to the inspiring place where Patrice O'Neal was at the end of his life: a place where mistakes gives birth to geniuses like Louis CK? It is an intriguing question. And it's a question all the world's coaches should ponder. Because the more people we get there, the more attractive football we get to witness. I really believe that. It starts with trust, and it ends (usually) with magic.

34 Beauty.

[Published in the GOAL number 7/2012]

Trying to analyze Rui Costa is like trying to analyze a sunset in Rio de Janeiro or a Shakespeare play. Not possible. Beautiful things are always difficult to describe; they must be experienced (preferably with a glass of red wine) in order to understand, but I will try with my limited language to tell the story of Rui Costa.

First: Rui Costa's DNA doesn't look like everyone else's. While ordinary people just try to get their body to move, Rui Costa's brain and body were always in perfect sync when he floated on the football field; a footballing Jesus, who generously spread joy to teammates in the shape of nanometer-precise passes, and long shots so well timed and clean that the goalkeeper rarely got a chance to react.

Wishy-washy? Well, I admit the introduction was a little bit hippie inspired. But I think that's how you best remember Rui Costa. Like artists such as Juan Carlos Valeron and Juan Roman Riquelme, it's not their trophy collections that make people like you and me remember them with a smile.

However, it would be a little ignorant to say that Rui Costa went completely trophy-less. How many will score the decisive penalty in a U20 World Cup? How many win the Italian Cup three times? How many will win the Champions League during his lifetime? And how many are loved in three different cities? Lisbon,

Florence, and Milan are all places where people in late hours have a tendency to be emotional when the elegant gentleman Rui Costa is mentioned – something the trequartista know about and appreciate:

> I say to myself that the strong links between me and the fans in the three clubs I represented are something that I am deeply grateful for today. Even now I can be shocked at how strongly some people feel about me.

Perhaps Rui Costa's peak in performance was in Fiorentina, where his partnership with Gabriel Batistuta was almost telepathic: Every movement that Batistuta made was felt by Costa; and each time Costa got the ball, Batigol had a sense of where he would move. Maybe he had his most successful stint in Milan, with the Serie A and Champions League titles as well as various other cups. And maybe he had his most emotional time in Benfica, where he returned in 2006 with hopes of more success than the cold reality could deliver (though he has done a fantastic job as sports director after his career as a player ended).

Of course we must finally mention his time with the Portuguese national team – a success story that could have been even more successful. He never won any championship at the senior level with his golden generation of Portugal, the sensationally talented group of players who spoiled Portugal in youth tournaments for more than two decades, and the senior national team thereafter.

Players like Figo, Abel Xavier, Jorge Costa, and Joao Pinto were all there that day when Portugal's golden generation was truly born, the last day of June 1991 – the day when Rui Costa stepped forward in front of 127,000 people at the Estadio de Luiz to take the decisive penalty in the U20 World Cup finals: "Even today I get shivers when I think of the explosive joy that followed after my penalty."

One day perhaps a new golden generation will be born in Portugal, an equally coherent and talented team like the original golden generation. And maybe a new reincarnation of Rui Costa, a new footballing Jesus, who can spoil us with beauty in a world that is not always so beautiful.

35 Luis Suarez and the laws of football (and life).

Sorry if I repeat myself, because I think this is a recurring theme in my texts: I love to take the easy road in life. Is there anything better? How happy are you when you manage to find a shortcut in Mario Cart? Or a child's version of *Crime and Punishment*? But it is, of course, not the advice I would give to my future son or daughter – especially if he or she wants to become a professional footballer. There's something that I think, despite my inbuilt laziness, is beautiful with football. You always have to prove yourself. All. The. Time. You can't operate like you do in poker and bluff a bad hand. It's impossible. It's easy to spot if someone has tried to ignore the laws of football, that is, a solid foundation is required to create something. When the film star Steve Martin was asked for his advice to younger colleagues, he said:

> When people ask me, "How do you make it in show business," or whatever, what I always tell them — and nobody ever takes note of it 'cuz it's not the answer they

wanted to hear... but I always say, "Be so good they can't ignore you."

Do you understand? Do you feel what I want to say? I see so many technical players strutting around on small five-o-side plans and make their fancy tricks in front of young children, and I have a feeling that for these people it is enough that they receive a comment like, "Wow, you must have played at a high level. I'm impressed. You could have become something." I'm somewhat similar. For me it is often enough to get a comment on my POTENTIAL greatness to make me happy. The problem with that is that it's just mental masturbation.

And that's why I love to watch Luis Suarez, who said that "when you come from the street, you need a high dose of ambition and strength to become a professional footballer." I even think I can become a better person by just looking at him play, like some kind of self-help, because he has some traits that I truly think I need. Dennis Bergkamp talked in his book *Stillness and Speed* about his time together with Suarez in Ajax:

> Of course you didn't always agree with everything that Suarez did, but he always tried to create something, he was always thinking in terms such as "How can I make the best of this situation?"

He is always testing new ways to terrorize the defense, and if the new methods don't work, he is modifying them during the match, which defenders hate because they know they will need to be both physically and mentally on top to be able to handle the battle against the energetic Uruguayan.

You can always erase a talented Adel Taraabt or Mario Balotelli from a match. Too lazy? I think so. And I hate that it is so, because I love them when they are at their best, and I wish they could always play like that. But players like them often disappoint me, probably because I see a couple of their faults in myself. The solution? Follow the laws of football and everything will be fine. And if you want help understanding them, look at Luis Suarez. He can't be ignored.

36 Hypothetically.

Suppose you are a skilled doctor á la Gregory House. You've figured out how to inject confidence in people, which is a revolutionary discovery, but there is a small problem with the whole procedure: In order to inject confidence in a man, you must first suck confidence from another person, as if the world's total self-confidence must be in a state of equilibrium. My question is: Which footballer in the world would you give confidence to and whom would you suck confidence from? How do you resonate? Would you like to see Tony Hibbert be megalomaniacal à la Dani Alves on Everton's right wing? Or would you love to see an even cockier version of Nicklas Bendtner?

37 Acceptance and patience.

What's wrong with us (somewhat aggressive start to the text Oscar...)? Because something is wrong with us. We football fans simply don't accept cycles. Once we have seen our team perform at their peak, we make that performance the norm. It's a little bit skewed. When my Arsenal had that season in 2003/2004, a season as close to perfection as a team basically can come, I didn't think: "Wow, this was something special. I am extremely happy that I got to experience this, but I am also aware that what I experienced was something unique." I rather thought: "Oh, this'll be the new standard. Cool. Let us now remain unbeaten in the league forever. That's reasonable."

A new generation is one of those things that make football interesting to watch. When a team reaches its zenith, it's time for new forces to first demolish part of the old foundation, but thereafter possibly even build a team with a higher zenith, who, like Ronald Reagan said, "stands on the previous generation's shoulders, with opportunities that didn't previously exist." It is exciting; it should be something that we fans embrace. And we should definitely not be shocked that new cycles occur, I mean, when has a team later managed to dominate (and I mean really dominate) for more than five years? It is of course theoretically possible, but in practice it just doesn't happen. Even a team like Barcelona experiences seasons where they lose to Bayern Munich 7-0 over two games. It is human, but humanity doesn't seem to interest us. We rather expect the continuous improvement of our team; otherwise we become bored, or worse, angry (or worse, depressed).

In all my years as a football fan, I haven't quite figured out how to process this. Acceptance? Maybe. But also a diminished interest in the results and trophies, how idealistic it may sound, could be a good idea. To see something new blossom should be a worthy enough activity for us football viewers. If you're smart, and I think that you are, you might hear that I am trying to argue for myself, because I'm not entirely happy with the fact that Arsenal has had something of a phobia for trophies the last decade. But I try to understand the greatness of growth; the excitement of exploring a new group of players' development and seeing which direction they take us. Buddha said, "The only permanent is change," because Buddha knew that tomorrow will never look the same as today –

something new arises in every second; every situation is unique in some way. If we accept that, the temporary pain we feel when Per Mertesacker slips won't hurt as much because we know that a new world is lurking around the corner. And there – which is fantastic – (almost) anything can happen.

38 Risk and chaos.

I was intrigued by a discussion between Gary Neville and Jamie Carragher during the fall of 2013, and I thought it would be worth digging into some parts of that conversation.

But first, a little background: During this period, Manchester United had one of their worst spell in decades, and the two ex-national team players explained how they experienced this United versus the classic United that Gary Neville was a part of. The most interesting part of the conversation was when Neville discussed what has always been United's strength, that is, the enormous pressure that they created during the last quarter of the game when they were chasing a deciding goal. Neville said that during his time, risk was always a key concept in the Manchester United dressing room: If you don't take risks, you win nothing. United used to take huge risks during the last quarter, just throwing every possible player into the offensive box, and in the end (sometimes with the help of the so-called "Fergie time") you could (almost) always check the live scores and see that United scored in the 94th minute. That this happened was of course no accident – it was a return on the huge risk they took.

Arsenal uses the same concept, but Arsene Wenger uses another language to articulate it: In interviews he usually talks about playing with or without the handbrake on. As long as the opponent hasn't scored, and as long as there are more than 20 minutes left in the game, Arsenal have a tendency to play with the handbrake on, but as soon as the game enters the final stage, or the opponents score, there's a shift in mentality, and suddenly it's the same United-chaos going on. The handbrake is gone.

Weaker teams are often risk-taking in the beginning of games: You see teams like Stoke and WBA apply high-intensity pressure from the start; they hope to shock the big teams early and then defend the lead. My theory is thus that a match between a big team and a smaller team usually has two really interesting periods, two periods of risk, i.e., the first fifteen minutes and the last twenty minutes, which means that in between we could spend some quality time with our family and friends; I mean, by streamlining the soccer process we could increase the chance of having stronger human relationships with the people that are close to us. Are you with me? Is there any sense in this thought? Or is part of the greatness of football that we invest our whole soul into the matches, both during funny and sad moments? That we tune in to the melancholy rhythms that often arise between minute 20 and minute 70.

I don't know how we ended up here after the initial premise, my brain is in chaos, and it feels like it is risky to continue to write, so I will stop here.

Live scores:
Öberg vs. United 0-1 94 mins

Öberg (mentally own goal)

39 About Sergio Busquets and hatred.

This text needs a quick background: I wrote it for Fotbollskanalen.se as a consequence of the intense El Clasico spring 2011, where Sergio Busquets in many ways had a lead role. And yes, I still feel a little uncomfortable when I hear Busquets name, but time heals wounds very effectively, so I can now see things from a different perspective. But enough about that – here comes the text!

[Posted on Fotbollskanalen.se May 11, 2011]

"Hate is too great a burden to bear. It harms the person who hates more than the hated," said Coretta Scott King, wife of Martin Luther King. Ergo: One should hate as little as possible.
I see this post as therapy for me. The thing is that I have some difficulties with the young man that I intend

to write about; sometimes my feelings are close to hatred. I know, it's crazy, but sometimes life is crazy and you act crazy. Actually, I'm rather a peaceful man who feels love for people in general. Sure, I've never been a fan of the likes of Hitler, Stalin, Mao, etc., but for the most part I smile when I meet a new person.

So why has it come to this? Why do I dislike this man Sergio Busquets so much?

Interesting question, of course, but let us first find out who Sergio Busquets is.

Just twenty kilometers from Barcelona, one of the approximately 200,000 inhabitants of Sabadell, Carles Busquets, became a proud 21-year-old father in 1988, when his wife gave birth to a boy who would be named Sergio.

Carles Busquets was a keeper, a rather successful one, who in the 1990s played second fiddle to Andoni Zubizarreta and Victor Baia for mighty FC Barcelona, which allowed his son Sergio already at an early age to have a natural relationship with the club that is supposed to be more than a club.

During his childhood, Sergio learned the official anthem Cant del Barça by heart; he was educated by the world's best passer, Josep Guardiola, and his father Carles told him all about the relationship between Barcelona and the capital team – and in Catalonia hated – Real Madrid. To first play in Barca and then switch to Real was unthinkable, somewhat like going down the same dark path that Anakin Skywalker did once a long, long time ago.

During adolescence, Busquets began to grow, not only as a football player but also length-wise. So, when he was 17 years old and had managed to infiltrate the Barca academy, he wasn't really molded in the same form as the hobbit mafia Xavi, Messi, Fabregas, Iniesta, etc. His passing game was certainly ok, but much of his strength was that he, perhaps due to his size and working-class background, was fearless on the field. He showed no opponent any exaggerated respect:

> I remember one game where people screamed all sorts of insults against us. Most of us were around 18-19 while opponents were men over 30 who wished they played for Barca, but it was no problem for me. I can

> deal with such situations. In fact, I like when it's a bit aggressive. I am, after all, a working class guy, but some of the other teammates didn't like the atmosphere.

And then he has a little of this Gareth Barry syndrome, that humble quality that makes all of his coaches scream with joy:

> My father taught me a lot about how to behave as a professional footballer: You have to work hard, be humble and listen to your coach. It sounds elementary, but I've seen a lot of really talented young people who left Barca because they had the wrong mentality.

When the current first-team coach Josep Guardiola picked up Busquets off Barcelona's reserve team in 2007, he probably thought, "Oh, this is gold: Here I have a player that plays simple, effective, and listens when I, the famous philosopher, speaks. He will go far."

A year later, Pep took over the first team and brought the young Busquets with him on the adventure. In September, he made his debut at the Nou Camp against Racing. Most people weren't much impressed by him, but most people don't know that much about football either. However, someone who probably knows more about football than most people is Johan Cruyff, the magic Dutchman, who was sitting in the stands and observed Carles' son. He was more than pleased with Barca's Xavi sidekick:

> He is technically superior to both Toure and Keita. His position game is almost perfect – both with and without the ball. With the ball he always manages to make the hard look very easy: he works almost exclusively with one or two touches on the ball. Without the ball, he gives us a lesson: to always be in right position so that he can effectively protect the team's back line and help the team more easily reclaim the ball. And all this despite the fact that he is young and inexperienced - not entirely unlike his coach (Pep) when he was young.

Since his debut, Busquets has been one of the first names on the team setup on one of the best teams of all time. He has won the league, the Champions League, the Euros, and also the biggest tournament of them all: the World Cup. And, he is only 22 years old. An ok resume to say the least.

But there's a side to Sergio Busquets that I, and probably quite a few others, have major problems with.

He is cynical. No, no, forgive me, wrong choice of words: he is ultra cynical. I mean, one could argue that he is the perfect player to have on your team, a player who literally does anything to win. A Brian de Bois-Guilbert (the nemesis of Ivanhoe). But even Guilbert had his code of honor. It doesn't seem like Busquets has one. He'll pull your shirt, rub your ankle when the referee doesn't see, whisper insults to you, and dive whenever he can. Many players do some of these things, but few manage to be an expert in all areas.

During the El Clasico weeks this all reached new heights. It started with a few less impressive dives, and ended with the alleged racist comments against Real Madrid's Marcelo. Even some of my friends, hardcore Barca fans, felt ashamed. Everything felt so ridiculous. It's a pity, because I like the player Sergio Busquets: He is both tactically and technically trained, a dream to have on your team. Maybe that's why I dislike him extra much, because he is so perfect otherwise.

Life is short, though, and I can't afford to hate; it's not healthy. But I can't deny that when someone mentions his name a feeling of discomfort arise in me.

Maybe some will say, "Don't hate the player, hate the game." Maybe they are right. But in that case, I definitely hate the game sometimes.

40 I criticize you only because I love you.

The exciting (exciting is here synonymous with crazy) Slovenian philosopher Slavoj Zizek, sometimes called the "Richard Pryor of philosophy," once uttered the words, "The one measure of love is: You can insult the other."

I don't know how it is for you, but I relate to this view, because criticism and questioning have been a big part of my relationships with family and friends. Giving criticism is of course something you do in the right context, and I have a feeling that some people sometimes use it in the wrong way with the wrong people. I mean, William Gallas shouldn't give criticism to Samir Nasri. They are French, they are sensitive and proud (stereotype alert!), which means that they have to be careful with what they say to each other. But let me say this: If we love someone and they love us back, there should be room to say virtually anything, as long as the other person has the feeling that there is love behind the words (which there probably wasn't the time William Gallas criticized Samir Nasri for "stealing" Thierry Henry's seat on the French team bus... sigh... why does it have to be so hard?). Because criticism really is, or at least can be, a declaration of love. If I love you, I also want you to be the best you can be – as Abraham Lincoln said, "He has a right to criticize, who has a heart to help." Therefore, people sometimes need a no-nonsense person in their life, a close human contact, like a grandmother who says "bullshit" when we take ourselves too seriously: someone who can stretch our mind and cut some layers of our ego.

This happens on football teams that know each other well. Sometimes I feel that a good atmosphere on a squad is translated into 23 smiling people, and I don't really like that translation. My translation would be that a good atmosphere on a squad means that everyone can express themselves freely without anyone else on the team taking offense, that there is an acceptance of challenging opinions, a bit like the atmosphere that Chelsea had during Jose Mourinho's first period with the club when the squad was filled with Zizek types like Michael Ballack, Didier Drogba, Arjen Robben, and John Terry; or the Arsenal team around 2003, when they had opinion machines such as Patrick Vieira, Martin Keown, Jens Lehmann, Fredrik Ljungberg, and Thierry Henry.

Maybe criticism is the wrong word; I have some mixed feelings about the concept. Maybe communication is a better word. But you know what I mean. A silent team is rarely a successful team – a constantly communicative team is probably on the right track. They care more about each other; they have broken down all barriers, all the overly polite tendencies that hinder authentic conversations, and have opened their hearts to criticism and, by extension, growth.

According to me, this is such an important component that I am surprised that it is not emphasized more in the media, but I'm not going to criticize: my love for the media is not strong enough for that.

41 I wanna be like Jürgen Klopp.

This text was written before Klopp moved away from Borussia Dortmund.

Through the better part of my life, I have looked for words or concepts that have been able to free me from the cultural norms of Umeå, Sweden, and the Western world. Sometimes I have succeeded; more often, I have failed. But I have always continued to look for new ways to see the world just as frantically as Arsene Wenger searches for yet another French talent.

The first time I encountered (not live, but on TV, just to clarify) Jürgen Klopp was sometime around 2005. I saw a Bundesliga match between Bayern Munich and Mainz, and I noticed that there was something special about Mainz's coach, but I could not at that time put into words what it was. A few years later I watched Klopp again, this time as the coach of Borussia Dortmund. Now I began to understand. It was not just his body language that was electric; it was the way he spoke in interviews: He was here and now, and he was thus able to respond spontaneously to all the questions he received. He finished each answer with a smile, sometimes even with a crazy laugh. Magical.

Since around 2009 I have followed Klopp very close. Yes, I'm not alone in that, but for me it hasn't just been to see Borussia Dortmund play energetic and fun soccer – for they do. But there has been an another dimension. I have seen Klopp as a guru, my Dumbledore, an enlightened man who tries to make himself heard in an often unenlightened world, and whose ideas challenge my way of viewing football.

One can see a common thread between my love for Klopp and my fascination with spiritual people such as Ram Dass, Alan Watts, George Costanza, and of course the laughing Buddha. The common denominator of all these wonderful enlightened beings is that they try to see beyond the words and concepts; beyond theories and science. It should be said that I am a big fan of good science (like the works of Carl Sagan and Richard Feynman), and good tactical discussions about Michael Carrick are pure joy for me (read my essay *In the mind of Gary Neville* and you'll understand), but when I hear someone talk about something outside the existing systems and structures of football, something a little bit out there, almost spiritual, I fall in love.

I had intended to share a couple of quotes by Klopp that I think describe his way of being pretty good, and that have helped me put words to my thoughts, but before I do that, I want to point out to the reader that these quotes aren't super original: There are of course others, both within and outside the football world, who have thought similar thoughts as Klopp. I will even try to connect his thoughts to other people's thoughts so as to not to make him any more unique than he already is. He can probably live with that. So, let's move forward on this Klopp journey by diving into quote 1:

Quote 1: "In terms of beauty and attractiveness, what I like is something a bit flawed, a bit rough. That's our game."

Listen, much of the stuff I do on a day-to-day basis is pretty mediocre, but I'm also pretty forgiving of myself; at least I try. But of course, it would be much easier if people in my immediate surroundings felt the same, that is, if they told me that it's ok to not be perfect. And of course, it would be great to have 14 or 15 Jürgen Klopps at my side (not literally... that would be creepy...) to enhance that feeling.

The Chinese philosopher Lin Yutang, who wrote the superb book *The Importance of Living*, which has one of the healthier world pictures I have encountered, argued that "Man is amazing in the way that she is by no means perfect, but she is perfect imperfect." This is the basis of Mr. Klopp's football philosophy. We are who we are, and if we let ourselves act freely, we will sometimes make fools of ourselves: Marco Reus will sometimes fail with a dribble; Ilkay Gundogan will occasionally make an error way too close to his own goal; and Mats Hummels will a couple of times per season give away a penalty to the opposing team.

But if you accept that everything can happen, you tell your players that mistakes can occur, and you even encourage risk-taking – then you open up a magical source. A sense of freedom spreads, a relief. This was something that the renowned American basketball coach John Wooden understood, and his classic expression "the team that makes the most mistakes usually wins" is like an extension of Klopp's quote above. Wooden won the NCAA college championship 10 times, which is something that probably would never have happened if he had chosen a more conservative sport psychology to use on his players.

Either way: The next quote will go into Klopp's view of limits and boundaries.

Quote 2: "I want us to be at the limit of what is possible each time we play. There's an old saying: 'A good horse only jumps as high as he has to.' Well I hate this saying more than anything. I think: 'A really good horse jumps as high as it can.'"

It's a good thought, perhaps especially for myself, because it is so far from how I reasoned and thought through much of my childhood. "Easiest possible way" has been my life's motto, and has been internalized in my soul for too many years: When asked to read *The Remainder of the Day*, I instead watched the (pretty boring) movie with Anthony Hopkins. That's just how a lazy person acts.

But with every passing year, I understand more and more the thrill of pushing yourself to the max. When I train, which actually happens more often than people think, I sometimes listen to the song *Can I Live?* by Jay-Z, and when he says the words "I'd rather die enormous than live dormant," I understand him better than a white guy from the upper middle class in Sweden should understand him, for there is something in that line that hits a nerve in me.

And this "jump as high as you can" feel has become stronger over the past decade in Sweden, since Zlatan Ibrahimovic had a breakthrough. He dares to be larger-than-life in a country that has never really been particularly comfortable with people who do more than what they are supposed to do; the people that go beyond the nine-to-five frame, the Swedish model (which in many ways is fantastic – no hatred intended), in the hope that there is something more out there. So, when Klopp tries to break boundaries, he also helps X number of people in their quest for self-realization. When his Dortmund jumps high, spectators are inspired to jump as high as they can. That must be good for the world in one way or another.

But let's go deeper: There is another dimension to the horse quote. When Klopp says "a really good horse jumps as high as it can," he has found a similarity between a horse and his team, that is to say, he has used an analogy. If you go to Wikipedia and search for "analogy," you will read how helpful they can be in teaching: "An analogy as used in teaching would be comparing a topic that students are already familiar with, with a new topic that is being introduced so that students can get a better understanding of the topic and relate back to previous knowledge."

And analogies are raised to the skies in cognitive scientist Douglas Hofstadter's book *Analogy as the Fuel and Fire of Thinking*, in which he argues that analogies are at the core of all human thinking.

Whatever you may think about analogies, they're usually a pretty good tool for making yourself understood. Instead of describing Mathieu Flamini as "a hard-working midfielder," I can instead write "He's a bit like an angry terrier, with the body language of a French commander, pretty similar to Napoleon," and thus make it easier for some readers to get a feel for the man.

Klopp is a master at using analogies, and even though they are sometimes far-fetched, you kind of understand what he wants to say. As when, after the Mario Götze transfer to Bayern, he made this analogy to the media in England: "Look, you work for the Guardian, and sometimes you see your colleagues and think, 'Oh no, the same old thing every day.' Maybe you want to go to the Sun? More money, less work. More photographs, fewer words." You think it's a bit far-fetched, but interesting, which means that you end up listening intensely and therefore more easily take in the message.

My brain is not in top shape right now, so I have no analogy to announce that we are now moving on to quote 3, which describes something that is important for all of us: using our hearts.

Quote 3: "'Next time, I will work with a little less of my heart,' I said because we all cried for a week. The city gave us a farewell party and it lasted a week. For a normal person that emotion is too much. I thought it's not healthy to work like this. But after one week at Dortmund, I was in the same situation again."

Here, Klopp talks about the time after he ended his coaching job in Mainz, and one can quickly conclude that he treats his clubs as a partner in a relationship. And you can also draw the conclusion that he goes into the relationship as wholeheartedly as Pippo Inzaghi once went into offside traps.

To join in with all our heart in something (whatever), to be vulnerable à la Klopp, is risky since we then close off some of our logic and let our emotions act freely. I'm not sure that I open my heart as often as I should, but it happens, and when I do it, I know that disappointment is lurking around the corner because I don't have any guard up. At the same time, I know of course on an intellectual level that it is probably even a greater risk to not make a "Klopp," that is to say, to treat your life with a closed heart; not to provide the opportunity for love to flow, because who will you then become? The Emperor in Star Wars? Tywin Lannister? Scrooge?

When you look at Borussia Dortmund play, it is like watching a Shakespeare play without knowing if it's a tragedy or comedy – we simply don't know where it will end. But one thing we do know is that we will be touched by Mr. Klopp's team: maybe it will be a shot from Reus that pumps our blood; maybe a tackle by Schmelzer, a dribble by Błaszczykowski (another one of these easily spelled Polish names in the world of football...), or a sprint by Grosskreutz. And maybe this is why we watch football? To be touched. Maybe football is the emotional machine that we need in a society that too often suffocates us in other contexts?

The psychologist and mystic Carl Jung argued that:

> One looks back with appreciation to the brilliant teachers, but with gratitude to those who touched our human feelings. The curriculum is so much raw material, but warmth is the vital element for the growing plant and for the soul of the child.

Well, you get the point. Knowledge will always be important... but it's the emotions that make the difference.

Quote 4: "The more you think about the individual, the more you will get back in return."

There's something that happens when you really try to understand another human being: to give them your whole presence; to listen with both ears; to cause that person to feel as important as Kanye West (or Nicklas Bendtner).

To illustrate with an example: Imagine you are at a dinner. You're tired, maybe even in a bad mood, and you also have wound up on the edge of the table next to a person who is as social as Nicholas Anelka. You have two choices: a) Either you sit there quietly during the entire dinner, then slip back home and watch an episode of Game of Thrones when it's finally over; or b) Try relentlessly to get the quiet person to open up. The risk is that you're going to waste some energy, but there is also a chance that the seemingly boring person actually provides some interesting thoughts back and suddenly creates a fire within you, an unexpected feeling of connectivity that makes the night a success.

So, what do I want to say with this? Well, Jürgen Klopp probably chose option b more often than option a.

The goalkeeper in Borussia Dortmund, Roman Weidenfeller, spoke in an interview about what it is like to go into Mr. Klopp's office for a conversation:

> You can talk about anything with him. He has an open ear and is always willing to listen. Though the conversation was awkward at first, you will always go out of his room and feel a little bit better.

That Klopp is thinking about the individual is also easy to see by his reactions after Shinji Kagawa and Mario

Götze were sold from Borussia Dortmund. When Kagawa left for United, they were both crying together in each other's arms for about twenty minutes, and when it became known that Götze had decided to sign with Bayern Munich, Klopp rang 6-7 of the Dortmund players who he knew would be heartbroken by Götze's departure. Something that probably wasn't in Klopps job description, but something that definitely needed to be done, according to him.

To remind the reader: I don't think Klopp is unique here. I know that even Carlo Ancelotti has this quality, that is to say, he is almost like some sort of father to his players. They love him. And of course there are several others who are skilled so-called "man-management" managers. But in a world where football coaches often try to keep some distance from their players, it is interesting, and to some extent quite liberating, to see that it is possible to lead people in a more intimate way.

Quote 5: ...

Understanding the truth is rather uninteresting; knowing it is of great importance; to live by it makes all the difference.

So it is one thing to hear Klopp talk about his concepts, but it's another to actually see him live in accordance with them, and therefore the last quote is a non-quote. Instead I want to emphasize here that the interesting thing to study is how Klopp interacts with other people: his way of speaking, his dress-code, his body language, etc. More than any other elite coach, Klopp distinguishes himself by sliding around with a big hoodie, messy beard, and a crazy smile. His movements on the sideline are widely known: He makes a fist so often that you may wonder if he is performing some kind of strengthening exercise for his finger muscles.

A German comedian recorded, after Borussia Dortmund's league title in 2011, the parody-song *I wanna be like Jürgen Klopp*, and besides being catchy (Usher's *Love in the Club* is sampled), there is also some truth in it. A large part of the German people, and some outside the country, probably know this. For there is something liberating to see a man acting authentically, following his instincts. Like Tarzan. Wilhelm Reich, a disciple of psychoanalyst Sigmund Freud, argued that Western ideas have a history of choking man's natural instincts, and this is something that must change if we are to get rid of the neurotic tendencies that our communities exhibit.

So let the spiritual revolution begin. This is my final message. Let us be like Jürgen Klopp.

Printed in Great Britain
by Amazon